CRUISING GUIDE FROM
LAKE MICHIGAN
TO KENTUCKY LAKE

CRUISING GUIDE FROM
LAKE MICHIGAN
TO KENTUCKY LAKE
The Heartland Rivers Route

By Captain Rick Rhodes

PELICAN PUBLISHING COMPANY
GRETNA 2002

Drawings by Pat Champagne
Photographs by author and Fred Lierley

ISBN 1-56554-995-3

Drawings are not for use in navigation.

Information in this guidebook is based on authoritative data available at the time of printing. Prices and hours of operation of businesses listed are subject to change without notice. Readers are asked to take this into account when consulting this guide.

Printed in the United States of America

Published by Pelican Publishing Company, Inc.
1000 Burmaster Street, Gretna, Louisiana 70053

Contents

Fred Lierley and our boat, *Free State*, in Chicago, our starting point

Introduction

My grandparents spent their entire lives in the Chicago area. My dad grew up on the northwest side of Chicago. Repeatedly, I too was drawn to the Midwest. From the late 1950s to the mid-1960s I lived in Louisville, Kentucky. In the mid-1970s, I was stationed at Fort Campbell, Kentucky—near the Land Between the Lakes and the southern terminus of this guide. Later, as an army reservist in the early 1980s, I spent the better part of one memorable summer stationed at one of those great river towns in northern Illinois. Again in 2000, I was drawn to the Midwest to research this cruising guide.

Circumstances could have been better for me in the early part of the year 2000. At that time, I was a middle-aged Peace Corps volunteer serving in Ecuador. Among scores of Third World frustrations, I contracted malaria. While I recuperated, it was determined that I also needed a shoulder operation. After the operation, the Peace Corps medically separated me that summer. For the first time in nearly two decades, I found myself unemployed. Another misfortune soon followed, when my 16-year-old Chevy van, and my post-Peace Corps abode, was totaled by an errant government vehicle.

After that last incident, I decided to visit respected cruising-guide writer Claiborne Young. Claiborne suggested that I travel to the Midwest and do the research for this guide. But first, I needed a boat. I favorably recollected a trailerable "pocket trawler," a 25-foot Nimble Nomad that I saw at a boat show in Washington, D.C. 10 years prior. In Maryland, I found and purchased a used Nomad. One good crew member was also needed. Fred Lierley proved to be an excellent one. Fred was another middle-aged and "departed early" ex-Peace Corps volunteer from Ecuador. In September 2000, Fred, I, and the Nomad hooked up in Chicago. Things soon improved. Fred and I field-researched this guide for many weeks. In November, Fred returned to Nebraska and his farm. I'm still living aboard my Nomad. And I trust you will be the beneficiary of our research.

Fred and I learned much while researching over 800 miles on Lake Michigan, the Calumet, Chicago, and Des Plaines waterways, and later the Illinois, Mississippi, Ohio, Cumberland, and Tennessee rivers. It was work; but we enjoyed it. We sincerely hope that you too will enjoy these great waterways and rivers in our Midwestern heartland. Our trip down these great rivers turned around my ill-started year. I trust, a trip for you will have a similar effect.

Book Organization

After the first four "preparation" chapters, this book is organized from points north to points south with a few exceptions (e.g., the farther-south Calumet River is addressed before the Chicago River). Nevertheless, if you are traveling in the opposite direction (from south to north), the 11 "regional chapters" are short and easy to follow.

Ocean sailors take note: the mileage throughout this guide is stated in statute rather than nautical miles. Eight statute miles is equivalent to about seven nautical miles. Facility locations, or the entrance points on the water to these facilities, are pinpointed by using the statute mile marker on that particular stretch of waterway, coupled with an indication as to which side of the river the facility is located on. In wider bodies of water (e.g., Lake Michigan and the Peoria lakes), GPS way points are used along with these mileage markers. Generally, if you plug in one of our GPS way points, you would have about a 180-degree safe semicircle of approach before arriving at that way point. Nonetheless, when approaching one of our GPS way points, do not neglect other common-sense cues (e.g., your depthfinder, obstructions on the water, and waterborne traffic).

Cautionary Note

In researching this guide, I expended great effort to ensure accuracy and provide you with the most up-to-date information. However, it is not possible to guarantee total accuracy. Nothing remains the same. Marinas, restaurants, other shore-side facilities, and the level of accommodations at marinas and restaurants change. Especially along these rivers, on-the-water navigational information such as shoals, the location of the channel, aids to navigation, and water depths are very changeable and fluctuate with the seasons, if not more often.

For navigating these rivers, the latest appropriate U.S. Army Corps of Engineers Chartbook Series is the present standard. These chart books are highly recommended. This guidebook is intended to be a supplement to these official U.S. government publications. Failure to follow the current on-the-rivers reality, even when it differs from the situation presented in this guide, can result in unfortunate accidents. We have worked hard to help minimize your risks and offer you options, but there are many potential hazards in any boating situation. Safe boating is ultimately in the hands of the captain and the crew. The author disclaims liability for loss or damage to persons or property that may occur as a result of interpreting information in this guidebook.

Pelican Publishing Company makes no guarantee as to the accuracy or reliability of the information contained within this guidebook and will not accept any liability for injuries or damages caused to the reader by following this data.

CRUISING GUIDE FROM
LAKE MICHIGAN
TO KENTUCKY LAKE

Spirit of Peoria, a modern paddlewheeler on the Peoria waterfront

CHAPTER 1

Life on the Rivers and Flooding

An Earlier Time

Native Americans are known to have lived on the Illinois River banks for 11,000 years. About 4,000 years ago, the Native Americans living in this area were making ceramics, trading with their neighbors, and building permanent villages. A little over a 1,000 years ago, the local inhabitants started cultivating crops, such as corn, squash, sunflower, and barley. About 1,000 years ago, a subtribe of the Illiniwek Indians, the Cahokia, built a city that covered about six square miles on the Mississippi River. In its heyday, from about A.D. 1100 to 1200, Cahokia, Illinois, across the river from present-day St. Louis, was occupied by 20,000 people. The Cahokia culture constructed earthen mounds with temples atop. This urban civilization rivaled the Mayan and Aztec civilizations in Central America and Mexico. The Cahokia Mounds State Historic Site preserves some of this culture's handiwork. Since the days of the Native American canoe, the Mississippi River and its tributaries were a great highway system throughout heartland America. The word "Messi-Sipi" in the Algonquin language translates closely to "father of the waters." The Mississippi River drains about 40 percent of the United States—from New York State (and the Allegheny River) to Montana (and the Missouri River).

European adventurers arrived in the Illinois River Valley in the late 1600s, attracted by rumors of a passage to the Far East and the Pacific. It is estimated that 6,000 Native Americans were living in the Illinois Valley around this time. In 1673, Frenchman Jacques Marquette, a Jesuit priest, and French-Canadian explorer Louis Joliet hoped to find such a route by water, overland, or a combination of both. Residing near the Straits of Mackinac, they had heard of a great river (i.e., the Mississippi) that flowed south.

Commissioned by the governor of French Canada, Count de Frontenac, the pair and five others started in Lake Michigan and proceeded to Green Bay, Wisconsin. Our explorers then took their two birchbark canoes up the Fox River and portaged over to the Wisconsin River. Then the team traveled down the Wisconsin River and discovered the mighty Mississippi River.

After eight days on the Mississippi, they encountered the friendly Peoria tribe. The Native Americans offered the explorers meals of roasted buffalo and dog meat. After meeting the Peoria Indians, they explored the Mississippi River as far south as the Arkansas River.

Near the Arkansas, the friendly local Native Americans convinced our intrepid explorers that, in fact, the Mississippi reached the known Gulf of Mexico, not the Pacific Ocean. Furthermore, the Native Americans informed them that the Indians were much less friendly closer to the Gulf of Mexico. The explorers would also be encroaching upon an unfriendly Spanish presence. So Marquette and Joliet turned around near the Arkansas River. On their northbound return trip, and heeding the advice of the local friendly Native Americans, they turned right at Grafton, Illinois and returned by an easier route—the Illinois River and toward the Great Lakes.

While on the Illinois River, between present-day Ottawa and Hennepin, Illinois, they encountered the hospitable Kaskaskia Indians. After a friendly encounter with the Kaskaskias, they proceeded to Green Bay, Wisconsin and back on Lake Michigan in September 1673. During their five-month, 2,500-mile canoe expedition, Marquette and Joliet got along well with the Native Americans. Marquette was a very pious man and proved to be motivated by the highest ideals of Christianity. But the great journey exacted a toll on him. Within the year, Marquette returned "to save" his Kaskaskia friends. In poor health, he died quietly on the banks of the Illinois River, nearly two years to the day after his great trip with Joliet started.

Joliet's luck was hardly better. In 1674 he was negotiating the last set of rapids before ending a trip in Montreal when his canoe capsized. Three companions were killed. Joliet survived after four unconscious hours in the water. But he had lost all of his exploration papers and his maps. Afterward, he redrew as much as he could from memory.

The next notable Frenchman to explore south down the Illinois River was Robert Cavalier Sieur de La Salle in 1678. La Salle was a dashing explorer, but arrogant, irrational, and paranoid. He had a history of not getting along well with his men.

Across the river from present-day Peoria, La Salle established Fort Crevecoeur. In 1680, while leaving Fort Crevecoeur for a return trip to Montreal, La Salle directed Belgian-born missionary Louis Hennepin and two companions to go down the Illinois River, then turn north on the Mississippi River and explore the upper reaches of the Mississippi. Hennepin made it as far as present-day Minneapolis. He was held captive by Indians, but after being freed, he returned to Lake Michigan by the same route Marquette and Joliet had departed the great lake eight years earlier.

In 1682, La Salle was the first European to reach the Gulf of Mexico from the north. He explored much of the lower Mississippi River basin. In 1685, La Salle claimed and named the area "Louisiana," after King Louis IV of France.

Later, La Salle planned to return to the Louisiana Territory with four ships and about 300 Frenchmen to colonize this area. The expedition was a disaster. After arriving in the Gulf of Mexico, they failed to find the mouth of the Mississippi River. One ship fell victim to Spanish corsairs. One ship gave up and returned to France. The other two ships overshot the Mississippi River and were later wrecked near Matagorda Bay and the La Vaca River on the Texas coast. The remaining and now very disgruntled "colonists" mutinied and murdered La Salle in 1687. A few of the remaining colonists were rescued from the Texas Gulf Coast in 1689. Today, on the Illinois River, we can sail past the towns of Joliet, La Salle, and Hennepin, as well as Fort Crevecoeur, and be reminded of these hardy explorers.

After the American Revolution, Eastern farmers and European immigrants began flooding into the agriculturally rich Illinois River Valley. Later, in 1836, construction on the Illinois and Michigan Canal began. The plan was to connect the Gulf of Mexico via the Mississippi River and parts of the Illinois River with a tiny Lake Michigan community called Chicago. This canal, thanks to immigrant laborers digging by hand, was completed in 1848. By the 1860s, a parallel railroad took over the canal's commerce. Nevertheless, the impact of the Illinois and Michigan Canal was great. Chicago was no longer a small hamlet, and the rich Illinois River Valley continued to develop agriculturally. Small cities and towns like Morris, Lockport, La Salle, Peru, Utica, and others sprang up along the canal.

Within about five years after Robert Fulton built the first successful steamboat, paddlewheel steamboats showed up around 1812 on the Mississippi River. In 1817, Henry Shreve designed the first really efficient Mississippi River paddlewheeler, the *George Washington*. The *George Washington* broke new ground by making a trip from Louisville, Kentucky to New Orleans in a mere nine days. And the return trip, fighting a stiff current, took a reasonably fast 24 days.

By the mid-1820s, 200 steamboats were plying the Mississippi River and its tributaries. Thanks to Mark Twain, we associate paddlewheelers with the Mississippi River. Nevertheless, one Ohio River boatyard supposedly built 6,000 paddlewheelers between 1820 and 1880.

The 20 years before the Civil War were the golden age of paddlewheelers. By the 1860s, there were nearly 1,000 steamboats on all these Midwestern rivers. But the life span of the steam-driven paddlewheelers was short. The Mississippi River was especially destructive to paddlewheelers, due to shifting sandbars, rapidly fluctuating water levels, and debris such as trees and limbs that were capa-

ble of gouging a hole in a hull and sinking a boat. The coal- and wood-fired boilers weren't safe either. There were catastrophic accidents. If that weren't bad enough, river pirates, often at night, boarded passenger boats and looted the entire complement. By the 1870s, the age of steamboats was quickly fading. By the dawn of the 20th century, the steamboat age had ended. The country's future looked west, and not along our north-south "heartland rivers." East-west transcontinental railroads were built, putting a further crimp in commercial steamboating.

During World War I, the railroads couldn't handle all the cargo. The government met this crisis by returning to the old water routes. Towboats and barges were built, and a channel was dredged on the Upper Mississippi and its major navigable tributaries. Locks and dams were also built. In the 1930s, the U.S. Army Corps of Engineers got into the act and built most of the present series of dams on the Mississippi River. Today, we are the beneficiaries of these great accomplishments . . . and this rich history.

Terrible Floods

These rivers have also flooded much throughout their existence. Each spring, melting snow and heavy rains swell the rivers. During the 20th century, floods were the number-one natural disaster in the United States as measured by lost lives and property damage. And these heartland rivers have claimed more than their fair share of victims.

In 1927, 26,000 square miles were inundated and the Mississippi River rose 57 feet at Cairo, Illinois. During this flood, the river broke through levees, 313 lives were lost, and 7,000 people lost their homes. After this disastrous flood, Congress provided and financed a system of flood control and the construction and maintenance of a nine-foot-deep, 400-foot-wide navigational channel on the Upper Mississippi River. This nine-foot depth was primarily achieved by building dams, backing up the water level. Other flood-control projects advanced around 1930 included levees, revetments protecting the levees, cutoff channels, and spillways. Today, you'll see many of these projects along our heartland rivers. Many of the standing older locks and dams were constructed in the 1930s.

Despite all of the safeguards, severe flooding still occurred. In January and February of 1937, the Ohio River experienced its worst flood of the century. It spilled over and Paducah, Kentucky was the victim, with water 61 feet over the normal level. Ninety percent of Paducah was inundated. In Cincinnati, about 450 miles up the Ohio River from Paducah, floodwaters crested at nearly 80 feet above flood stage. During the 20th century, Cincinnati "saw" the over-60-foot mark on the Ohio River 21 times. During that 1937 flood, which lasted for a couple of weeks, the Ohio flooded, then receded, and then flooded again. All Ohio River towns, from Pittsburgh to Cairo, Illinois, were ravaged. Around 400 people lost their lives, 1 million people were left homeless, and property losses were in excess of $500 million.

In May of 1983, there was a flood due to excessive rain in the central and northeastern Mississippi River region, wreaking another $500 million in damages. Ten years later, heavy rains began in April and contin-

ued through the summer. Much of the area remained flooded or was under the threat of flooding from May until September 1993. During this damnable flood, 50 lives were lost, 72,000 homes were damaged, and damage to property and crops reached around $20 billion. The water rose 22 feet above flood stage and 36,000 square miles were affected. In Grafton, Illinois the high-water mark was 20 feet above the roadway, which in turn was about 20 feet above the current river level. One hundred buildings were lost in Grafton and 95 percent of the local businesses were shut down. Many people called this horrible flood of 1993 a 100-year flood. When the Mississippi River was flooding, certain tributaries, like the Illinois River, were dammed by flood waters and were unable to drain normally. These tributaries also flooded their banks, and there were even reports of some rivers reversing their direction due to the intense pressure coming from the Mississippi River.

Another regional flood struck Portage des Sioux, Missouri only two years later. In May 1995, damage was estimated to be between $5 and $6 billion. We've been told that spring 2000 was the first time in many years that the marina buildings in Portage des Sioux did not get flooded. Near Kimmswick, Missouri the Mississippi River rose over 40 feet in this 1995 flood.

In March 1997, a slow-moving storm front dropped 10 inches of rain in the Ohio River Basin. The foot of the Ohio rose over 22 feet in nine days and remained that high or higher for another 23 days. In 2001, the Mississippi River in northern Illinois once again experienced severe flooding. The third-highest river crest on record, at over 22 feet, was recorded in late April 2001.

I've heard that near St. Louis, the flow on the Mississippi can increase by 25 times in cubic feet per minute (CFM). For this to happen, the river level must grow significantly higher and the river current must flow considerably faster. In a year when there is no major flooding, the Mississippi River still carries 400 million tons of soil to the Gulf of Mexico, enough to cover 3,240 square miles one inch thick—or the states of Delaware and Rhode Island combined.

Barge traffic near the Ohio River Bridge at Cairo

CHAPTER 2

Towboat Appreciation and Etiquette

In the United States today there are about 25,000 miles of navigable waterways. These waterways carry about 3,750 towboats. Annually, U.S. inland rivers support 21,000 barges and transport about 1.4 billion metric tons. The Ohio River alone is estimated to carry about 100 million tons of all types of freight each year. The Rivers and Harbors Act of 1930 started much of the work on the present navigable waterway in the Upper Mississippi River region. Since the opening of a nine-foot channel during the 1930s on the Middle Mississippi River, towboat tonnage has increased by approximately 10.5 percent each year since 1938.

The configuration of barges tied together is called a "tow." The very biggest tows on the Calumet and Chicago Sanitary and Ship Canal consist of about eight barges (two barges wide by four barges long). On the lower Illinois River, a typical tow is three by five, or 15 barges. Fifteen barges is equivalent to two and a half freight trains or two and three-quarters miles of railcars.

The rivalry that started last century between barge and rail exists to the present day. A typical towboat, pushing a tow, might consume 2,400 gallons of fuel per day. But this converts to about one ton of cargo being moved 500 miles on only one gallon of fuel! Towboat interests claim that the diesel exhaust emissions of towboats are 35 to 60 percent that of locomotives and trucks per ton mile, and river transportation is the most environmentally friendly form of transporting goods. The carrying capacity of 15 barges is the same as about 900 semitrailers or nearly 12 miles of tractor-trailers.

Barge configurations usually double in capacity on the Mississippi River. We commonly saw 30-barge configurations (five wide by six deep). I've even heard of some bigger on the lower Mississippi River—as big as nine by nine (i.e., 81 barges being push by one towboat)!

The typical horsepower (HP) of these towboats is 4,000 HP. The bigger ones can be 7,000 or even 10,500 HP. The length of a towboat can vary between 50 and 200 feet. The barges usually connect to the towboat at two large towing knees that are integrally constructed as part of the bow of a towboat. Once a tow gets under way, it's on a 24-hour-per-day schedule, with a typical complement of 12 persons.

Most individual cargo barges are 35 feet wide by 195 feet long. A three-by-three barge configuration fits nicely, and with practically no room to spare, in a 600-foot-long by 110-foot-wide locking pit. Some individual barges are vertically tapered like a boat on one end. But many barges are squared off at both the bow and stern ends. The taper on the bow of a barge is called the "rake." If multiple barges are connected "in line," it's much more fuel efficient for the pushing towboat if the squared ends (i.e., ends without any rake) meet in the middle of the tow. The raked ends are most efficient at the very front and at the very back of the tow configuration.

Tows on these rivers are suited for and carry bulk commodities and petroleum products. The largest single bulk commodities are the grains (e.g., corn, wheat, oats, barley, and rye), petroleum products (fuel oils, lubricating oils, kerosene, and gasoline), coal, and coke. Most of our nation's coal moves by barge. Agricultural goods account for about 70 per-cent of barge cargoes. Agricultural commodities are loaded onto the empty barges from one of the many riverside grain elevators.

These products are generally going down-river, to near New Orleans, and then loaded aboard oceangoing ships. Thanks to Midwestern barges, the per-ton cost of trans-porting corn is the lowest in the world. In

Tow and barge hatches

A towboat pushing a small petroleum barge up a river

1998, about 60 million tons of grain traveled down the Mississippi River to New Orleans, before continuing on to markets all over the world.

Many of the petroleum products are headed in the opposite direction, upriver from the oilfields of Texas and Louisiana. Coal is often shipped upriver from the coal fields of southern Illinois and western Kentucky. Some other bulk commodities carried on the tows include iron, scrap iron, steel, aluminum, cement, sulfur, fertilizers, sugar, and dehydrated molasses. Don't ever think of anchoring in the channel on any of these rivers, as you'd most certainly be struck down by a tow in the middle of the night.

Towboat operators generally refer to smaller vessels or recreational boats as RVers—as in recreational vessels. When an RVer is going to meet a tow, we highly recommend making VHF radio contact. On these rivers, monitoring VHF 13 is probably better than VHF 16. Dual monitoring capability would be even better (i.e., VHF 13 and 16). Besides, if you listen to channel 13 enough, you can hear the conversation of those barge captains and invariably you'll develop an appreciation and an empathy for their weighty responsibility.

Port-to-port passing is the first conventional choice in a meeting situation, but be extremely flexible here. Many times a starboard-to-starboard encounter with a tow is the much better option. I would guess that we passed port-to-port more than half of the time, but perhaps had starboard-to-starboard encounters about 40 percent of the time. A tow may be taking, or anticipating a need to take, a bend in the river wide, and it could very well make more sense for a starboard-to-starboard encounter. A towboat may also be weighing other traffic ahead that would affect the side on which they'd prefer to pass you. You should attempt to ascertain, via radio contact with the tow, which side is best for the encounter. Towboat captains will often reply something like, "I'll meet you on the one whistle," or "I'll pass you on the two whistle." One whistle means *their port* side, or a port-side-to-port-side encounter when meeting head-on. Likewise, the two whistle means *their starboard* side, or a starboard-to-starboard-side encounter. On the busy Mississippi River, many towboat captains shortened this jargon even more to "I'll meet you on the *one*" or "I'll see you on *two*." One means their port, and two denotes their starboard.

I've heard recreational boaters complain that towboat captains sometimes don't respond on the VHF radio, when the RVer tries to hail the tow. One contributor to this problem is that these towboats all know each other's vessel's name and we, RVers, usually don't. We can't do much about this. But towboats are more apt to know their location on the river in relation to a river light, island, bridge, shoal area, power plant, industrial dock, or the like. RVers are more likely to know their location on the river by the mile marker. On the VHF, a towboat is less likely to respond to "hailing the southbound tow near mile 928" and more likely to respond to "hailing the southbound tow near Ledbetter Light," even though they are both the exact same location. Even if RVers do everything "properly," some towboats still will not talk to them. Towboats often have their own darn jargon for everything. For example, I heard one on the radio saying that he was "coming out of the canyon." Well, there is no darn canyon on any chart. What did he mean? Us RVers don't know where "his canyon" is located.

In conditions of reduced visibility or bad water (i.e., high or low level of river water), there is a higher probability of encountering a northbound, upriver tow than a southbound, downriver tow. Upriver tows are usually running empty and are much lighter and more maneuverable. Southbound tows are usually full and have less maneuverability when traveling with the current.

Towboat pilots have blind spots that generally extend for several hundred feet in front of, and to the sides of, barges. Bringing a towboat to a stop can take a mile and a half. Five short blasts signal immediate danger.

These guys, the towboat captains and crew, are hardworking professionals. Let's give them their rightful right of way. A respectful and cordial relationship, and perhaps garnering some knowledge from their river anecdotes, will likely enrich our own trip on these heartland rivers.

A deep lock opening up after a drop

CHAPTER 3

Locks and Bridges

Locking Your Boat Through

On a trip from Lake Michigan to Kentucky Lake, you'll likely encounter 13 locks. There are nine locks on the Illinois Waterway, but you'll likely bypass one depending on how you depart Lake Michigan (i.e., either the Chicago River Lock or the Thomas O'Brien Lock on the Calumet River). The Mississippi and Ohio rivers have two locks each. You'd lock down in the last two locks of the Mississippi River, but you'd be locking up in the lowest two locks of the Ohio River. Then you'd lock up 57 feet in either the Kentucky Lake Lock on the Tennessee River or the Lake Barkley Lock on the Cumberland River. If you continued south to Mobile, Alabama on the Tennessee-Tombigbee Waterway, you'd lock up one more time at Pickwick Landing Lock and Dam on the Tennessee River, and then start locking down, a total of 12 times, after you arrived on the Tenn-Tom Waterway. The sketches in this chapter present vertical profiles of the 26 locks between Lake Michigan and Mobile, Alabama.

The water level behind the locks is known as the pool level or simply "pool." The pool generally extends to the next lock and dam. References to water levels are pegged to some particular pool level. This is usually the normal pool level. The terms spring pool (typically higher water) or winter pool (typically lower water) are also sometimes used.

Besides water depth, specified bridge clearances are also pegged to the pool level. If the water is lower than the stated pool, there is slightly more bridge clearance. If the water is higher than the stated pool, there may be dangerously less overhead clearance than shown on the Corps of Engineers charts. Bridges, not always but often, also have a "yardstick" on the waterline near a bridge piling. These present a fairly accurate height from the water level to the overhead clearance. You can also use this information to determine the difference between the "yardstick" clearance and the stated clearance on the Corps charts. For example, you notice the water level under the bridge is 38 feet below the bridge clearance. On the Corps charts, the normal pool under this bridge is listed at 36 feet. Now you know you have two feet more height clearance than the stated pool level for other bridges in that same pool, and possibly other pools nearby (but also two feet less depth).

Pool length is another river concept. There is usually slack water in the pool behind a lock and dam. This has often had a beneficial effect on fish and other wildlife by expanding and enhancing the riverine habitat.

Locking a boat has the potential to be dangerous. We've never witnessed a mishap in a lock, but we have heard of several. We heard that just outside the Chain of Rocks Lock on the Mississippi, the wake from a tow knocked a high-priced sailboat into riprap shore, causing thousands of dollars in damage. Another towboat-RV incident occurred just outside the Lockport Lock on the Illinois River years ago. A tow maneuvering into the lock crunched a sailboat parked just outside the lock. We

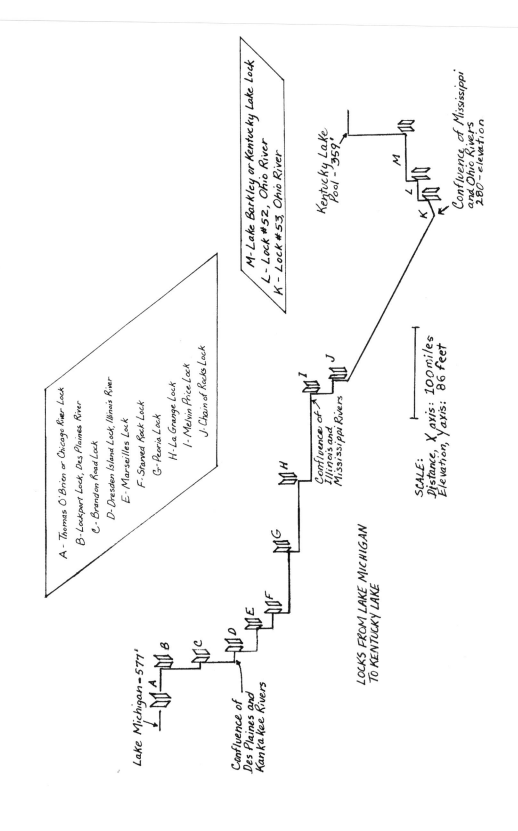

Lake Michigan = 577'

A - Thomas O'Brien or Chicago River Lock
B - Lockport Lock, Des Plaines River
C - Brandon Road Lock
D - Dresden Island Lock, Illinois River
E - Marseilles Lock
F - Starved Rock Lock
G - Peoria Lock
H - La Grange Lock
I - Melvin Price Lock
J - Chain of Rocks Lock

M - Lake Barkley or Kentucky Lake Lock
L - Lock #52, Ohio River
K - Lock #53, Ohio River

Confluence of Des Plaines and Kankakee Rivers

Confluence of Illinois and Mississippi Rivers

LOCKS FROM LAKE MICHIGAN
TO KENTUCKY LAKE

Kentucky Lake
Pool - 359'

Confluence of Mississippi
and Ohio Rivers
280 - elevation

SCALE:
Distance, X axis: 100 miles
Elevation, Y axis: 86 feet

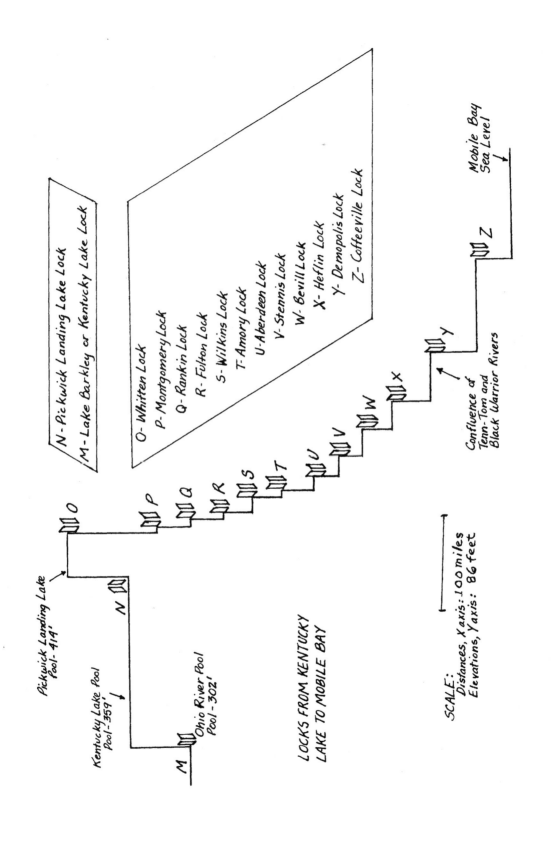

LOCKS FROM KENTUCKY
LAKE TO MOBILE BAY

M - Lake Barkley or Kentucky Lake Lock
N - Pickwick Landing Lake Lock
O - Whitten Lock
P - Montgomery Lock
Q - Rankin Lock
R - Fulton Lock
S - Wilkins Lock
T - Amory Lock
U - Aberdeen Lock
V - Stennis Lock
W - Bevill Lock
X - Heflin Lock
Y - Demopolis Lock
Z - Coffeeville Lock

Pickwick Landing Lake
Pool - 414'

Kentucky Lake Pool - 359'

Ohio River Pool - 302'

Confluence of
Tenn-Tom and
Black Warrior Rivers

Mobile Bay
Sea Level

SCALE:
Distances, X axis: 100 miles
Elevations, Y axis: 86 feet

heard one story of a downriver-bound house-boat captain not seeing the dam ahead on the lower Ohio River. Luckily, the houseboat captain smartly had his VHF radio tuned on and heard some other boater on the radio relay, "Look at that houseboat—it's about to go over the dam." He realized that the boater was talking about him! He quickly took corrective actions, saved his boat, and then found the lock.

In another incident, soon after a crowded lock opened on the Tenn-Tom Waterway, a sport fishermen in the rear of the lock came barreling out. His discourteous wake caused another boat to slam on the bottom just outside the lock. Thousands of dollars of damage ensued as the slammed boat had two bent struts, two damaged props, and two damaged rudders. Despite hightailing away from the lock and the crime scene, the sport fisherman didn't get away with it. The Alabama State Patrol cornered him in the next lock. Waking other boats is always discourteous, but it can be downright costly and even criminal behavior. Around locks, the potential for damage is often worse.

Now that I've scared you about the danger near locks, I've felt that I have done my job. If you learn some of the locking basics and etiquette, you will almost certainly have no problems. Even if other boaters around you mishandle themselves, you'll still be able to cope. On the other hand, going through or even anticipating a lock can break the routine. Some people even think locks are fun.

There are restricted boating areas, upriver and downriver from the dams. Dam-related turbulence, such as unusually strong currents and undertows, can and do create hazardous conditions for small boats in these areas.

These hazardous areas are usually marked with orange and white danger buoys.

Oftentimes large concrete and steel federal mooring cells will be seen in the vicinity of locks. These are primarily there to help secure barges and towboats near the locks. We also saw these mooring cells (back East, they are sometimes called "dolphins") near the confluence of two waterways. While waiting for a lock, and when there was no barge traffic in the area, we sometimes loosely attached a line from our vessel through an eye on one of these mooring cells. A boat fender, or two, may also be needed if you are attaching yourself to a mooring cell while awaiting a lock opening.

I'd recommend having a few boat projects lined up (and ones that you could drop quickly) if you anticipate a relatively long delay outside a lock (e.g., splicing some frayed lines, marine-texing a few gel-coat scratches, cleaning debris from the bilge strainer, sweeping the cabin sole, or tightening deck rail screws). It has generally been our experience that when lock tenders say that it will be a half-hour wait, it often means a wait of an hour and a half. The waiting period can only be an estimate, and the lock tenders probably give you their "most optimistic" assessment. There are times when we had waiting periods nearing a couple of hours, and then there were a few times when we were lucky and were able to enter immediately into the locking pit.

There is a vessel locking priority: 1) U.S. government vessels; 2) commercial passenger vessels; 3) towboats; and lastly 4) recreational vessels. Near locks, we observed a few U.S. government vessels and no commercial passenger vessels, but of course we saw many towboats. We were told that on the Illinois River, a recreational boat might have to wait as long as three lockings in one direction, deferring to the towboat traffic. Considering river traffic coming from both directions, this could possibly be a wait for six lockings. We have heard of recreational vessels waiting as long as 10 hours on the Illinois River. I think this seldom happens, but the possibility does exist.

In a typical 600-foot-long by 110-foot-wide locking pit on the Illinois River, a three-by-five tow configuration will need to break apart into two sections to "lock through." Each individual barge is 35 feet wide and 195 feet long. After both barge sections and the push boat lock through, they will need to retie outside the lock. This is when those federal mooring cells serve their purpose. The barge section that is unaccompanied by the towboat can safely moor itself to those federal mooring cells.

Just because you are outside of the lock, don't assume the lock will open for you. It is always recommended that you make VHF radio contact. Several years ago during a trip down the Atlantic Intracoastal Waterway in Florida, I learned a good VHF radio lesson. My sailboat was last in a four-boat caravan awaiting a drawbridge opening. The lead boat hailed the bridge tender on the VHF and requested the opening. Unbelievably, after the third boat cleared the bridge, the open span started coming down. Immediately, I swerved hard to port and luckily avoided—by only a few feet—having my mast crunched under the closing drawbridge. Afterward, I had some choice words for the inattentive bridge tender. But nevertheless, I should have used my VHF earlier and not assumed that this bridge ten-

der was looking at what was obvious to me— four boats. From that day on, whether the first boat, in the middle, or the last boat, I always try to make radio contact with any bridge or lock tender.

Each lock has a VHF hailing channel (usually VHF 13 or 14) and sometimes the tender can also be reached on VHF 16. After initial radio contact is made on their hailing channel, lock tenders often wish to switch their "standing by" traffic to another working channel. Besides having a VHF radio, lock tenders also have a telephone land line. These telephone numbers as well as the VHF channels are provided in this guide. If you don't have a radio, some locks (e.g., O'Brien Lock on the Calumet River) have lock attention devices on the lock guide wall (pull cords that attach to buzzers or bell signals, etc.). Another way to get the lockmaster's attention is with a horn signal. The appropriate horn signal is a long blast followed by a short blast.

Locks also have red-yellow-green visual traffic signals. Sometimes these signals are hard to find on the lock guide wall. Red means stay out; the lock is not ready. The yellow signal sometimes isn't used. When it is, it means that the lock is being made ready— recreational vessels may approach the guide wall but must not enter the lock. The green signal means the lock is ready for recreational vessels and you may enter the locking pit. Green and yellow lights on at the same time are supposed to mean "the gates cannot be fully opened, but the vessel may enter with caution." When you are entering or leaving a lock, the lock tender may also use blast horn signals. There are nuances, but one or two long blasts means it's OK to enter (or leave) the pit.

A government dredge in a raised lock

Several boats entering a lock to lock down

Before a vessel enters the locking pit, all crew on deck should be wearing life jackets. This is a legal requirement while in the pit. Boat fenders should be out to protect the sides of the boat from the slimy, rough concrete walls. When entering or leaving the pit, stay in channel and away from the orange and white danger buoys. Always enter and leave the locking pit at a "no wake" speed.

After the Chicago or Calumet rivers, all of the locks on the Illinois River should provide and throw you two lines from near the top of the locking pit. But this is not the norm on the Mississippi, Ohio, Tennessee, or Cumberland rivers. On these rivers, one or two sets of 50-foot dock lines need to be supplied from your own boat. On the Mississippi, Tennessee, and Cumberland rivers, there may be floating mooring bits or check pins to secure your boat. Unless you are tied to a floating bollard or mooring bit, you should not securely fasten any dock line to your boat. Instead, you should be able to gradually pay out (when dropping) or snug up (when lifting) these lines, properly working the slack in or out. I like snubbing the dock line a half a turn around a boat cleat for a little tension and taking the slack up or letting it out between the cleat and my hand. If you use one line, tying up at amidship is best.

On the Ohio River, which has the oldest locks, there are no lock-supplied lines nor floating mooring bits. You will need to secure a long line to your vessel and then heave this line to the lock tender or his assistant. The lock tender will loop your long line somewhere above the lockwall and then throw the bitter end of the line back down to you and your boat. While lifting or dropping, you would adjust the slack near the bitter end of

this line. When the lift or drop is complete, you'd pull the bitter end of your line through the lockwall attachment point and gather the entire line back to your boat.

Those two locks on the lower Ohio River are quite old and sometimes have more turbulence in the pit than found in other locking pits. The Ohio River Lock plumbing and valves are less sophisticated than some of the newer locks. There may be fewer and very big valves; these bigger valves create more turbulence than many and smaller, newer valves.

The lowest two locks on the Illinois River, the Peoria and the La Grange locks, and the two locks on lower Ohio River have a "high-water sailing line." If river water level is naturally high enough, the locks can be bypassed. The dams are older wicket dams, and they can be lowered. When the dams are lowered into the riverbed, vessels can safely sail over the high-water sailing line on the "open river" and over the lowered dam instead of using the locks. If you are lucky enough to bypass a lowered dam, beware—there will likely be a stiffer-than-normal current over river constriction attributed to this lowered dam.

If the locking pit has floating bollards, use your own line, and put a wrap or two around the bollard from a cleat amidship. If you don't already have them, it's best to install some amidship cleats, and with solid metal or delrin cleat backing plates. Locks with floating bollards nestled in the lockwall are common on the Tennessee and Cumberland rivers and the Tenn-Tom Waterway. Most locks on the Tenn-Tom have about 10 floating bollards (i.e., room for 10 recreational boats), but don't be surprised if not all 10 are properly functioning. On the other hand, the relatively new Lake Barkley Lock has 14

Construction at the Olmsted Lock on the Ohio River

A lock opening up near St. Louis

floating bollards, and all are usually in work-ing order.

If you are locking down, it seldom matters where you tie up. Often, but not always, there is next to no turbulence anywhere in the pit when locking down. When you are locking up, the front of the lock sometimes has less turbulence than the rear when the pit is filling. Most of the relatively new locks (e.g., Lake Barkley) have very little turbulence either when locking up or down. The older locks have more turbulence. Many times the lock tenders will direct you where to tie up: on your port or on your starboard side, and at the front or at the rear of the pit. And obviously, this depends on where other boats ahead of you have already tied up. When you make contact with the lock tender, ask him where you should tie up. If there is room, he will more than likely position you in the area of the pit where the turbulence is minimal.

Don't ever tie up your vessel to a ladder or other immovable object in the locking pit. Surprising as this sounds, lock tenders have relayed stories of recreational vessels doing just this. The result can be catastrophic. Engines should be turned off because it's diffi-cult to dissipate the exhaust fumes in a lock-ing chamber. Any movement aboard the deck should be limited to that which is essential.

Before departing the lock, wait until the lock gates are completely open and the lock tender gives you permission to depart. The vessels nearest to the exiting lock gate, even if they are the slower vessels, should get out of the pit first. Passing other boats in the lock is not permitted, unless instructed by the lock tender. If there are many boats in the locking pit, and they travel at different speeds, it's good etiquette and safe boating for the slower boats to pull over, slow

down, or even wait just outside of the lock, thereby letting the faster boats pass in a con-trolled setting outside of the locking pit. If you lock your recreational vessel with a tow and barge, you will likely be directed to be the last one in, after the tow, and the first one out, before the towboat negotiates out of the pit. If the lock tender has been professional, and by far most are, and if there is not much VHF traf-fic, I like to get on the radio and "thank" the lock tender for "his hospitality" after I've departed.

I have found that lock tenders are generally the most knowledgeable and helpful folks on their portion of the river. They are undoubt-edly one of the best reservoirs of local river knowledge. If you treat them respectfully, and they are not too busy, they'll generally answer many of your "river questions." A few times, I have even heard of recreational boaters ask-ing the lock tenders about possibilities to tie up somewhere on the outside of the lockwall area overnight, and being granted permission.

Encountering Bridges

There are more than 170 bridges between Lake Michigan and Kentucky Lake or Lake Barkley. Slightly more than 100 of these bridges are located in the Chicago area alone. By far, most of these bridges are "non-obsta-cles." But, depending on your overhead clear-ance, there may be some bridges that merit concern.

There are generally four types of bridges on these rivers: (1) fixed, (2) bascule (which is the typical drawbridge), (3) lift, and (4) swing. Fixed bridges are just that. They cannot open. They are often of a higher clearance than the other bridges and support interstates, large roadways, or heavy-traffic highways. Bascule, or draw, bridges are most often associated with city streets. These are often older bridges and they have counterweights to balance the raised roadway section. When a bascule bridge is open, the clearance near the center of the bridge is virtually limitless. Lift bridges are commonly seen on railroads and on a few roadways. Two towers are near each end of the lift section. The bridge section lifts parallel to the water with counterweights in each tower. Lift bridges, when open, do not have a limitless overhead clearance. The open clearance is only as high as near the top of those towers. Swing bridges have no towers nor counterweights. There is usually a substantial pier near the middle of the river. The bridge will swing open, but will stay parallel to the water, from this central pier. Unlike lift bridges, the overhead clearance on swing bridges is limitless. But there does need to be sufficient room, both downstream and upstream, for the swinging sections to extend out over the water.

On the Illinois waterways, there are some older bascule and lift bridges that are no longer operational. And it turns out that these often limit overhead clearance. Besides the bridges, there are many over-the-river power lines, cables, pipelines, and even conveyors. The overhead clearance of these obstructions is higher than any nearby un-opening bridge. The Corps of Engineers chart books usually present the clearance information on these other overhead structures as well as the bridges.

The heaviest concentration of bridges is

A raised railroad lift bridge on the lower Illinois

The tower of a lift bridge on the lower Illinois

near the entrance of the Chicago River. There are 20 bridges in the first two and a half miles. These bridges arc nearly all roadway drawbridges, more technically known as bascule bridges. The lowest-clearance bridge is a railroad lift bridge with only about 10 feet above normal pool on the main Chicago River channel. Nearly all of the bascule roadway bridges on the Chicago River have about 17 feet of overhead clearance in the closed position. These bridges do open up for boats requiring more clearance, but not usually on demand. This would be too disruptive to the downtown Chicago Loop traffic. Furthermore, these downtown Chicago River bridges are manned by teams of roving bridge tenders who hopscotch from one bridge to another bridge farther along the route. A good way to get a hold of these roving tenders is VHF 12. There are also several phone numbers you can try: (a) (312) 744-8700 (the bridge lift coordinator),

or (b) (312) 745-3112 or (312) 745-3113 (the superintendent of bridges), or (c) (312) 744-4280 (the Lake Shore Drive Bridge, 7:00 A.M.-3:00 P.M.), or (d) (312) 744-4200 (the 24-hour phone number).

In the fall and spring, organized flotillas, sometimes several per week, negotiate underneath these opening bridges. A few good sources for finding out more about the schedule of bridge-opening flotillas in this area are Crowley's Yacht Yard, (312) 225-2170, and the Lake Shore Drive bridge tender, (312) 744-4200. On the Chicago River, and after the opening bascule bridges, there are still other *un-opening* bridges limiting the overhead clearance to only 17 feet. Please refer to the first table in chapter 7 for these Chicago River bridges.

An alternative route south out of Lake Michigan is the Calumet River. Un-opening or fixed bridge clearances on the Calumet are

A lift bridge on the Calumet

higher than on the Chicago River—about 24 feet. Nevertheless, about 25 miles past the first 24-foot bridge, and three miles past the confluence of the Chicago and Calumet channels, there is an un-opening railroad bridge with a clearance of only 19 feet, thereby limiting the Calumet alternative to only 19 feet of clearance. Please refer to the second bridge table in chapter 7 for these lower Chicago Sanitary and Ship Canal bridges.

About 40 miles out of Lake Michigan, and on the Des Plaines River in Joliet, Illinois, there are six low bridges. Five of these bridges are bascule roadway bridges. In their closed position, the lowest bascule roadway bridge clearance is 16 feet. All of these Joliet bridges open, but unusually these drawbridges have a

posted "open" height of about 47 feet. Joliet also has one especially dangerous railroad lift bridge with a closed clearance of only nine feet and an open lift clearance of about 50 feet. You'll find these Joliet bridges in the bridge table information in chapter 8.

After Joliet, the bridge clearance challenge fades significantly. Beyond Grafton and off the Illinois River, the bridges on the Mississippi, Ohio, lower Cumberland, and lower Tennessee rivers are all fixed with substantial overhead clearance (i.e., at no less than 57 feet, and oftentimes with much higher clearances). Farther south, according to the Corps of Engineers charts, the lowest un-opening bridges on the Tennessee River as well as the Tenn-Tom Waterway are 52 feet at normal pool.

Bridge tenders typically monitor VHF channel 16, but you may also find them working on VHF channel 12. Many bridge tenders also have land-line telephone numbers. There are 11 tables in this guide that depict bridge information by chapter.

Most of this information was garnered, synthesized, and simplified from the Corps of Engineers charts. Some Illinois-area information was provided by Laura Cannell at Marine Navigation Incorporated, the Great Lakes *U.S. Coast Pilot* (edition 2001), NOAA charts, and through direct telephone calls to various sources (e.g., nearby lock masters, the superintendent of bridges in Chicago, etc.). On the Illinois waterways, sometimes the bridge height information conflicted among the Corps of Engineer charts, NOAA charts, and the *Coast Pilot*. After the Chicago area, if the discrepancy was close (i.e., within two feet), or the bridge clearance was sufficiently high, I tried to present the more conservative bridge height figure. There were some instances where the discrepancy was much greater, and even different types of bridges were cited for the same bridge crossing. In these cases, and when my memory couldn't reinforce the veracity, I footnoted the more doubtful choice, although the footnoted information could just be correct. The bridge tables on the Illinois waterways (i.e., for chapters 6, 7, 8, 9, 10, and 11) have an "Unimpeded Vertical Clearance" column. After the Illinois waterways (i.e., chapters 12, 13, 14, and 15), the bridges are all fixed bridges and this previous column would add no useful information. In these latter chapters, if appropriate, this column was replaced by a "regulated high water level," or eliminated completely. We also highlighted in bold type those "potentially limiting" bridges on the Illinois waterways.

If you are suspicious or have a very small margin of space between your boat height and the posted bridge clearance, you should double check with that particular bridge before negotiating your vessel beneath it. The current pool stage is another variable that significantly affects the clearance height. The pool stage fluctuates at least seasonally and monthly, and it can fluctuate even more frequently—weekly or even daily. Hence, the information in our bridge tables, especially the clearance data, is designed to help you and provide you with relative comparisons. For related reasons, we did not present "inches" on bridge clearances. We rounded the bridge clearances down to the nearest whole foot. If you are "pushing the envelope" and needing those extra inches under the bridge clearances, other common sense and more comprehensive additional assessments are necessary (e.g., reading the "waterline yardstick," consulting with the bridge tender, carefully factoring in the current pool level, etc.) before proceeding beneath a questionable bridge.

The junction buoy at the Ohio and Cumberland rivers

CHAPTER 4

Reading Charts and Buoys, Planning Ahead, and Confronting Fog

Charts and Buoys

There are six sets of chart books covering these heartland rivers and Chicago's Lake Michigan. The National Oceanic and Atmospheric Administration (NOAA) produces the Lake Michigan/Chicago area chart book—14926. NOAA individual charts 14927, 14928, and 14929 also cover this area. On NOAA charts, the buoys are indicated with reasonable accuracy. NOAA charts also depict water depth.

The U.S. Corps of Engineers provides five chart books on these rivers. Buoys may or may not be shown on Corps of Engineers chart books. Likewise, water depths are not shown on Corps charts. Nevertheless, the channels of Corps waterways should be maintained to a nine-foot depth. Some Corps chart books are much better than others. One maddening thing about using the different sets of Corps chart books is that about 40 percent of the legends and symbols are different from one Corps District chart to the next. Also unlike NOAA charts, Corps charts vary much in quality and presentation. In my opinion, the U.S. Army Corps of Engineers District out of Nashville (i.e., producing the Tennessee and Cumberland river charts) has the best set of chart books. Appendix A of this guide lists these specific chart books and charts.

As in all of North America, the buoyage system on these rivers is the IALA Maritime Buoyage for Region B. Simply put, that means red, right, returning. Returning is going upstream. You'd pass the red buoys on your right side when going upstream. If we are taking a trip from Chicago to Cairo, Illinois, we are going the opposite way, or downstream, on all these rivers. So staying inside the marked channel and going downstream, the green buoys would be passed on our right side and the red buoys would be passed on our left side.

Unlike on the East Coast tributaries, most buoys on these rivers do not have numbers. The buoys get knocked and moved around too much, and the river channels shift frequently. Hence there is logic not "to bed" the buoys to a specific "spot" on a river channel. A Corps chart may show five buoys around a bend, and there may actually only be three, or vice versa.

Red buoys are commonly in the shape of a nun (i.e., with a pointed top) and green buoys are commonly in the shape of a floating can (i.e., with a flat top). On Peoria and Upper Peoria lakes, tall fixed concrete structures also mark the Illinois River channel. On the banks, there may also be red and green daymarks.

Another type of buoy is the red and green junction buoy, or even the red and green shoreside daymark. Two-colored buoys or daymarks indicate a junction between two navigable rivers. Ashore at Fort Defiance, south of Cairo, Illinois, you'll find a red and green junction daymark marking the junction of the Ohio and Mississippi rivers. The "preferred" (or more traveled) channel correlates to the topmost color of that daymark or buoy. At Point Cairo, the daymark is red over green. Going upriver, the Mississippi veers left and the Ohio goes to the right. Hence, that topmost red color of the daymark would indicate that the main channel veers to the left (i.e., the Mississippi River channel).

I believe that buoy spotting is easier on wider and more open bodies of water. Spotting buoys on these rivers is a tad more difficult because the background "visual shore noise" is nearer and it exists nearly everywhere. There are many daymarks on the shore, and you can't spot them until you're close to or even with them. Here you don't have that visual sweep that you'd have on larger bodies of water. You'll often see these little white placards on daymarks and even trees that mark the mileage on the particular river.

Planning Ahead

All recreational boats should have a VHF radio. A radio is essential on these rivers. VHF channel 16 is the International Distress as well as a common hailing channel. VHF channel 13 is also very important. Depending on the river, most towboats monitor VHF channel 13. On these rivers, we found it more practical and informative to be monitoring VHF channel 13 unless we needed to speak to a bridge tender who was on VHF 12 or 16. By monitoring channel 13, we had a handle on the towboat traffic movement near us. This was considerably more practical information than anything we could have garnered by listening to VHF channel 16. We also communicated with the towboats on channel 13. Channels 12 and 14 are often used as the working channel for many river locks. Some

of the more sophisticated marinas have their own favorite working VHF channels.

Naturally every boat should have a working depthfinder. Corps of Engineers charts do not show depths like NOAA charts. Nevertheless, the Corps should be maintaining the channel depth to nine feet. If you find your depth soundings rapidly decreasing, you most likely have strayed away from the channel. Slow down, turn around, and backtrack your way to the channel. You could not do this very well without a depthfinder. A depthfinder with a shallow-water audio alarm is especially good. Most of us don't, nor should we, have our eyes affixed to the depthfinder. But if we accidentally meander out of the deep water, an audio alarm followed by corrective action can keep us from grounding.

We also feel that it is imperative for every boat to have a compass. Furthermore, in this guide we sometimes describe a location using compass variables (e.g., the Eastport Marina is situated near the southeast corner of Peoria Lake). If you're not as directionally intuitive as some pros, you may need to look at your compass to find out where is that "southeast corner." One spring night on the Potomac River and in heavy fog, I was able to navigate nearly blind for about five miles solely by using my compass and depthfinder. Eventually, I lost the channel and anchored out for the remainder of the night, and until the fog cleared the following morning.

We have provided you with 33 GPS way points in this guide. GPS units are more useful on larger open bodies of water than on these rivers. Nevertheless, a GPS unit still has practicality here. With a GPS unit, you can do fun things like get your boat speed over the ground, determine which direction (besides downriver) you are traveling, figure out an ETA for your next "landfall," determine the distance you have traveled, and more. GPS way points are also nice "targets" to aim for, especially in the large bodies of water and where the shoreline may become lost or confusing. In open large bodies of water, I don't believe that one should navigate solely by GPS, and much less so on these rivers. Nevertheless, the 33 GPS way points provided in this guide should be useful for finding shoreside facilities on the larger bodies of water (e.g., Lake Michigan and the Peoria lakes). We also threw in a few other "interesting" GPS way points (e.g., at the confluence of major rivers).

Our GPS latitude/longitude way points were calibrated to degrees, minutes, and 100ths of minutes. Be careful; some folks calibrate their GPS units to degrees/minutes/seconds. A second is a 60th (not a 100th) of a minute. The difference between 37.50.59N in 100ths and 37.50.59N in seconds is nearly 800 yards, or almost half a statute mile.

If you have a 33-foot sailboat, with a cradled 55-foot mast on the deck, remember, you are now a 55-foot boat. And this can become really dicey in the locks. I'm certain that a few sailors have scraped the ends of their mast while maneuvering in a locking pit.

Somewhere around or before Chicago, a sailboat will need to have its mast unstepped, or lowered, to make it underneath the 17- or 19-foot fixed bridge clearances around Chicago. Many sailboats securely affix their "downed mast" to the deck and later step the mast in either the Kentucky Lake area (if it's

less than 52 high) or in the Mobile area (if it's taller than 52 feet high).

One of our unexpected last-minute purchases was a one-eighth-inch piece of brass rod stock. It was to be used as propeller shear-pin material to replace anticipated sheared dinghy prop pins. We also ended up cutting pieces from it and shaping these for a myriad of applications. That soft brass rod proved quite handy. As far as clothing goes, don't forget the raingear.

Along the rivers north of St. Louis, many restaurants, grocery stores, hardware stores (and auto parts stores), laundromats, a Walmart, and even a hot tub can be found. If you are able to park your boat for a half-hour or longer at lunch or dinnertime at any small town on the Illinois River, it's impossible to go wrong with a local meal. Just about anywhere between Morris and Grafton, Illinois, you have an excellent chance of finding a quality and delicious three-course meal, with a salad and a dessert, at unbeatable prices at any local eatery. This is especially true if you order the daily special. Just call it Illinois hospitality.

Libraries (with usually free Internet access) can also be found in most of these same Illinois towns. Some of the towns that we would recommend as great stopovers are Morris, Seneca, Ottawa, La Salle, Peru, Hennepin, Henry, Lacon, Chillicothe, Pekin, Havana, Beardstown, Meredosia, Kampsville, Hardin, and Grafton. The frequency of friendly, accessible, small river towns starts to dwindle south of Grafton. Nevertheless, there are still a few great ones ahead—Portage des Sioux and Kimmswick in Missouri, Metropolis on the Ohio River in Illinois, and Grand Rivers in Kentucky.

If you yearn for the urban cosmopolitan scene, you will be enthralled with Michigan Avenue in the Chicago Loop area. Forget accessing St. Louis by boat. However, Joliet, Peoria, and Alton, Illinois as well as Paducah, Kentucky are all very delightful small cities. They offer a host of accommodations and a variety of activities. We wouldn't recommend passing up any of these four great cities.

Safe anchoring locations along these rivers are much more limited than on Eastern bays, estuaries, and wide rivers. You need to plan where you hope to end up each evening, even if it is at anchor, so you don't have to boat at night. We recommend a destination plan for each day. Know your boat's typical daily travel range; figure where you might be tomorrow evening in a best-case scenario (e.g., the maximum possible distance covered). Find a marina or anchorage in that vicinity. Then, we recommend planning backwards looking for alternative marinas or anchorages, finding anywhere between two and near a half-dozen alternative stops, before your farthest-distance scenario. If you make your—perhaps flexible—goal, celebrate with a good drink after the boat is safely secured for the night at a marina or at anchor.

Confronting Fog

As fog poses a threat to motorists on land, it poses a special threat to boaters navigating on these rivers. Fog occurs when warm air laden with moisture cools down. Warmer air is capable of holding more water vapor than cooler air. When the warmer air cools, the once invisible water vapor held in it condenses from a gas to a liquid state. The liquid is still suspended in the air and these small suspended liquid droplets create the fog that obstructs our visibility.

The most prudent course in fog is to wait it out. It's also a good idea to listen to the upriver and downriver towboat captains over the VHF to ascertain what the fog is doing a few miles up- or downriver. It may have lifted over you, but you could get sopped in only a mile downriver. This happened to us, after we departed too early one morning.

In foggy conditions, a boat could easily collide with something dangerous. A towboat could run over an unseen recreational vessel. Visibility in fog is much worse than nighttime visibility. At night, if it's not foggy, lights can usually be seen at a distance away. In fog, this isn't true. In July 1956, the Italian luxury liner *Andrea Doria* was broadsided by the *Stockholm* in fog outside New York Harbor. The liner sank, and 51 lives were lost. Radar provides a boat with another sense of perception in fog. But in 1956, both the *Andrea Doria* and the *Stockholm* had radar and something still went badly amiss.

The likelihood of fog on these rivers is greatest during the fall and spring. Throughout the fall, the fog on these rivers will likely get worse, week by week. As the early morning temperatures become progressively colder, the air's capacity to produce morning fog also becomes greater. Beware, because especially on these rivers, it might be clear over the land but dangerously foggy over the river. Radiant heat from the morning sun will usually "burn off" early morning fog. If you must move in impaired-visibility conditions, having a radar, slowing down, listening for barge traffic on the VHF,

Fog in the diversion channel south of Cape Girardeau (on the Mississippi)

and utilizing sound-producing devices improve your chances of getting through the fog.

On a positive note, having made long sailing trips on much of the East Coast and to the northwestern Caribbean, I found that I had to—and it was smart to—lose many traveling days because of bad, or predicted bad, weather and sea conditions (strong cold fronts, rough seas, storms, etc.). Traveling on these heartland rivers, except for a partially lost day on account of morning fog, one usually doesn't have to lose those "weather days," as you prudently

need to do in so many other boating situations.

The Great Circle Cruise

The north end of Lake Michigan connects to Lake Huron and the other Great Lakes at the Straits of Mackinac. The eastern Great Lakes connect to the Hudson River and the Atlantic Ocean via the New York State Barge Canal (the old Erie Canal route). The Saint Lawrence River also connects to the Hudson River via waterways connected to Lake Champlain. Both New York's Hudson River and Quebec's Saint Lawrence River have

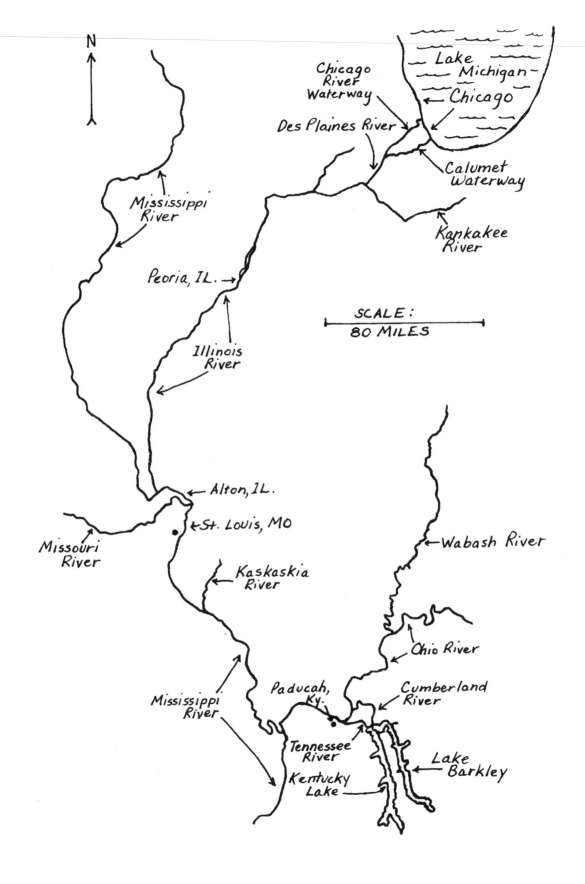

been 350-year-old tried and true navigable waterways to the Atlantic Ocean. Nowadays, the largest of recreational vessels can also leave Lake Michigan and Chicago from the south end, and generally head south to reach the Gulf of Mexico and the Atlantic Ocean.

Mobile, Alabama usually anchors the southwestern corner of the Great Circle. Florida, and perhaps as far south as the Florida Keys, is the southeast corner of this great circle. Albany, New York, or perhaps points even farther north or east, is in the northeastern realm of this circle. And Lake Michigan and Chicago are at the heartbeat near the northwest corner of this Great Circle cruise. By way of some great heartland rivers, a recreational boat can travel south from Lake Michigan at 577 feet above sea level to the Gulf of Mexico. A trip from Chicago to the Gulf is just under 1,300 miles, and from near latitude 42N to near latitude 30N. This guide will take you halfway there, from Chicago to Western Kentucky, or about a 700-mile-long trip. And, most importantly, we will offer you many options along the way. Worldwide, there are probably a handful of Great Circle cruises (e.g., a circumnavigation of the globe, or of South America, or of Africa, or even within the Caribbean). But this just may be the only Great Circle cruise in the world where you are not handicapped by lacking the knowledge of a foreign language.

Many different types of recreational vessels—trawlers, sailboats, sportfishermen, houseboats, and even small powerboats—are making at least a portion of this Great Circle cruise. Some boats are professionally captained, while others have a novice captain and crew. Many different-size boats make the trip or a portion of it—from the multimillion-dollar megayachts to small trailerable runabouts. We made our trip in a "small" 25-foot trailerable Nimble Nomad "pocket trawler" with a 50 HP two-stroke Yamaha outboard motor.

As far as boating accommodations along the rivers, we have tried to be inclusive. We've addressed the gamut of facilities, from those small obscure boat ramps (that are used by small trailerable boats) to the first-class marinas facilities and yacht clubs having "all of the fixings" and the ability to lavishly host those megayachts.

What's Next?

The first four chapters of this guide were designed to give you an appreciation and a flavor for these great heartland rivers and to offer some background information for planning the journey. Now, the fun really begins. We are about to make a trip from Chicago's Lakefront to Kentucky Lake. Please review the overview drawing of this trip. The following 11 chapters will segment this trip in logical bite-size regional chunks. Please read on.

Mooring in Monroe Harbor, beneath the Standard Oil Building

CHAPTER 5

The Chicago Waterfront and Lake Michigan

Chicago, our nation's third largest city, sits on the southwestern corner of Lake Michigan. There are many marinas in this corner of the lake. And there are also two routes out of the lake to choose from as you start your southbound journey. The Chicago River leaves the lake south of the Navy Pier in the heart of downtown Chicago. The entrance to the Calumet River is about 12 miles to the southsoutheast of the Chicago River entrance and near the Indiana-Illinois border. The Chicago River and Calumet River channels connect to each other about 30 miles from Lake Michigan. Which route should you choose leaving Lake Michigan? It depends. It's hard to describe the feeling of going through the skyscraper canyon of downtown Chicago. But on the Chicago River, you may be limited by more restrictive bridges (less spacing between bridges, lower bridge clearances, and more restrictive openings). And beyond the first five stimulating miles, the Chicago River-Chicago Sanitary and Ship Canal becomes quite bland. The Calumet River has slightly higher bridge clearances and less restrictive openings and is marginally a more pleasant river past the first seven industrial miles. See the drawing for these alternative routes out of Chicago and down to Joliet, 40 miles out of Lake Michigan. Read on; the choice is yours.

But before you proceed into either the Calumet or Chicago River, let's talk about some facilities on that Chicago Lakefront. The city of Chicago has 29 miles of lakefront shoreline, but we'll limit our lakefront marinas to a swath of about 18 miles in the heart of Chicagoland and on the southwest corner of Lake Michigan. There are many other nice marinas outside of this swath. You can learn more about these other marinas in the Lakeland Boating Lake Michigan guide.

On Lake Michigan, three marinas are less than five miles north of the Chicago River entrance. Six marinas are between the Chicago River and Calumet River entrances, and Hammond Marina, in Indiana, is about two miles south of the Calumet River entrance. With the exception of Hammond Marina, all of these marinas are part of the Chicago Park District, (312) 747-0737, and operated by Westrec Marinas. All of these marinas monitor VHF radio channels 16 and 9, but they should switch you to another working channel after initial contact. See the excerpts here from the NOAA charts in the Lake Michigan area. NOAA chart excerpts in this guide are the only ones that depict water depths.

The three marinas north of the Chicago River are Montrose Harbor Marina, Belmont Harbor Marina, and Diversey Harbor Marina. All three are close to the same size. Montrose Harbor has about 370 slips and is home to the Corinthian Yacht Club. Belmont Harbor houses both the Belmont Yacht Club and Chicago Yacht Club. It also has a crane service for small boats. You need to be able to pass beneath an 11-foot bridge to enter Diversey Harbor, thus limiting this marina to powerboats. Lincoln Park and its zoo are

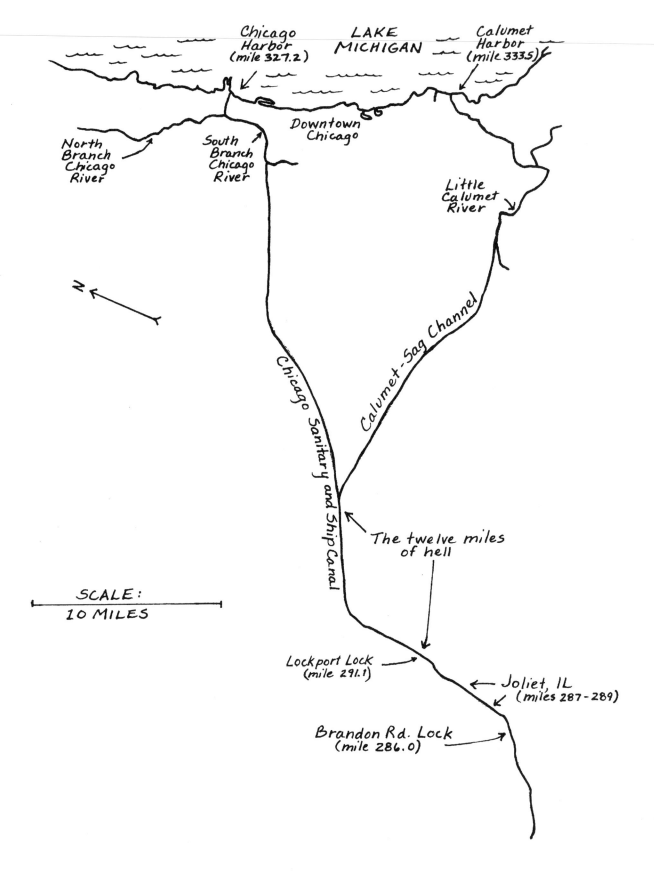

across the street from Diversey Harbor. Fuel is sold at Diversey Harbor but by the Diversey Harbor Yacht Club, not the marina. Besides floating docks, all three of these marinas have many moorings as well as unattached "stardocks" in their harbors. A stardock needs to be reached via dinghy. A typical stardock can hold about 16 boats with all of the boats' bows pointing inward and toward the center. The stardock is moored to the bottom but not attached to the shore.

Montrose Harbor Marina (312) 742-7527; VHF 71

Accepts transients—yes (3-7-day advance notice
    may be required)
Floating steel docks—yes
Dockside power connections—30 amp
Dockside water connections—yes
Waste pump-out—yes

Belmont Harbor Marina (312) 742-7673; VHF 69

Accepts transients—space-available basis
Floating steel docks—yes
Dockside power connections—30 and 50 amp
Dockside water connections—yes
Waste pump-out—yes
Gasoline—yes
Diesel fuel—yes
Ship's store—yes (small)
Restaurant—nearby

Diversey Harbor Marina (312) 742-7762; VHF 69

Accepts transients—yes
Floating steel docks—yes
Dockside power connections—30 amp
Dockside water connections—yes
Waste pump-out—yes
Gasoline—yes, call yacht club at (773) 929-8819
Diesel fuel—yes, call yacht club at (773) 929-8819
Boat ramp—yes

Chicago Harbor, about three miles south of Diversey Harbor Marina, is a huge harbor just outside downtown and at the entrance to the Chicago River. The famed Navy Pier contains 50 acres of promenades, parks, restaurants, shops, various amusements, and some waterborne activities (mostly charter boats). The pier extends more than a half-mile into Lake Michigan. You can't miss it. A breakwater with openings, nearly three miles long, envelops the Navy Pier and the entrance to the Chicago River. Our GPS way point outside the main break in this wall, and nearest to the Chicago River entry, is 41.53.29N/87.35.36W. Our GPS way point near the entrance to Monroe Harbor Marina and Du Sable Harbor, the closest marinas to the heart of downtown Chicago, is 41.52.41N/87.36.48W.

Everything in Monroe Harbor is on a mooring. As a transient, you'd be directed to one of more than a thousand mooring floats. If you take a mooring, you will need to call a harbor tender on VHF 68 or phone (312) 742-7659 to arrange for a trip to shore aboard a tender. The Chicago Yacht Club is also inside, near the northwest corner of Monroe Harbor. The yacht club may or may not have a temporary slip for a transient boater.

Du Sable Harbor Marina, a separate marina facility with over 400 slips, is attached to the northern end of Monroe Harbor. You can only enter Du Sable Harbor after you are already in Monroe Harbor. This is different from what is depicted on NOAA charts 14926 or 14928. There is a break in the seawall in the northeastern corner of Monroe Harbor that connects to Du Sable

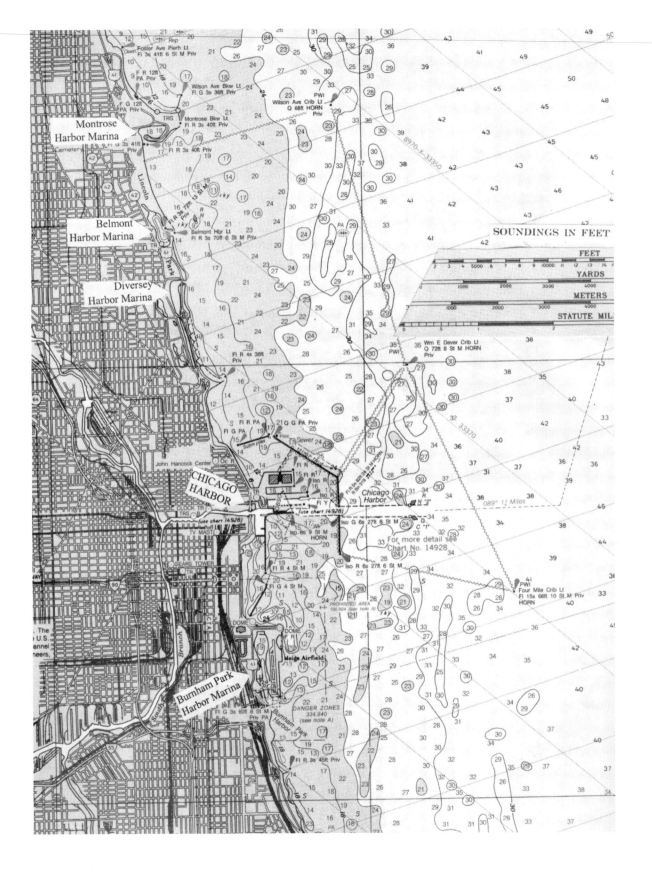

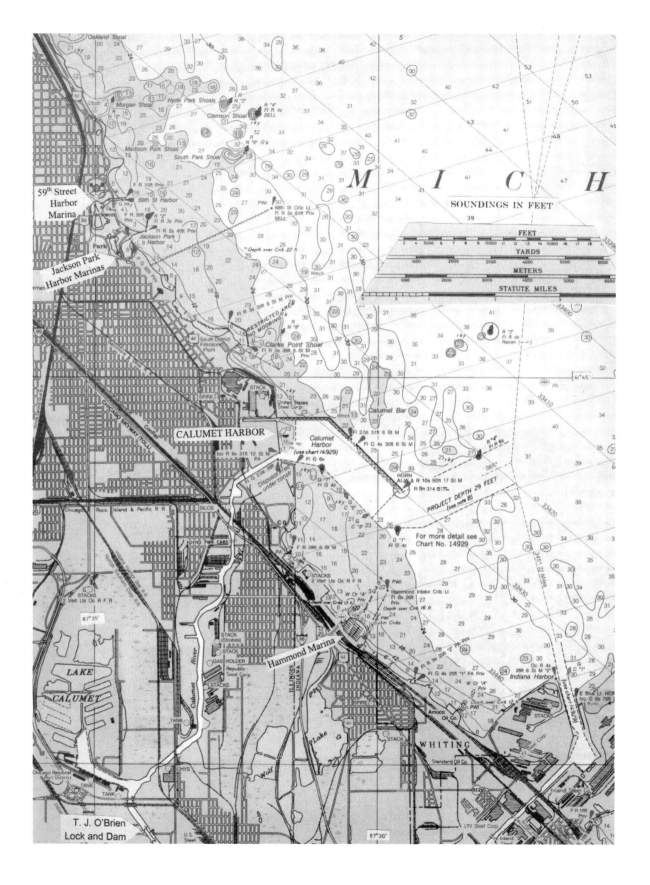

Harbor. The marina's namesake is Jean Baptiste Du Sable. Du Sable was born in Haiti, of a French father and a black-Haitian mother, and was likely born as a free man. Many consider this fascinating man of many skills the father of Chicago. In the 1770s, Du Sable settled near the entrance to the Chicago River with his Indian wife. The British imprisoned him during the American Revolution because of his loyalty to the French and the Americans.

The Columbia Yacht Club, and its large immobile ship, is housed between Du Sable and Monroe Harbor. If you are moored in Monroe Harbor or berthed in Du Sable Harbor, you have about a five-block walk to Michigan Avenue and the Chicago Loop area. This section of Chicago has many fine restaurants, five-star hotels, and historical landmarks. There are also over 40 museums in central Chicago. Grant Park is also across the road from Monroe Harbor. A small grocer, Grand Food Mart, is nearby on the lowest level of Randolph Street.

Monroe Harbor and Grant Park

THE CHICAGO WATERFRONT AND LAKE MICHIGAN 51

Monroe Harbor Marina (312) 742-7643; VHF 68

Accepts transients—space-available basis
Floating moorings—yes
Waste pump-out—yes
Showers—yes
Restaurant—several nearby

Du Sable Harbor Marina (312) 742-3577; VHF 67

Accepts transients—yes
Floating wooden piers—yes
Dockside power connections—twin 30 and
    50 amp
Dockside water connections—yes
Waste pump-out—yes
Showers—yes
Ship's store—yes
Restaurant—several nearby

Back on Lake Michigan, you can't miss the Adler Planetarium about a half-mile south of the entrance to Monroe Harbor. This planetarium is at the north end of Meigs Field. The entrance to Burnham Park Harbor Marina, the largest facility on this portion of the Chicago Lakefront, is less than two miles south of the entrance to Monroe Harbor Marina entrance and less than a mile south of the Adler Planetarium. Besides its 1,100 slips, immense Burnham Park Harbor Marina has about a dozen stardocks and scores of moorings. You'd enter the complex from the south near GPS way point 41.50.89N/87.36.34W. It's also hard to overlook McCormick Place, which sits near the southwest entry. McCormick Place is the largest indoor convention center in the country, with 2.2 million square feet. The harbor's namesake, David Hudson Burnham, designed much of modern-day Chicago about a hundred years ago, and in particular the Loop Area and the city parks along Lake Michigan. Once you entered the Burnham Park Harbor channel and headed north, you'd be passing two fields. Merrill Meigs Airfield is to your east, and Soldier Field, home of "Da Bears," is to your west. The Burnham Park Yacht Club has a restaurant located in the marina.

**Burnham Park Harbor Marina (312) 747-7009;
    VHF 71**

Accepts transients—yes
Floating steel docks—yes
Dockside power connections—30 and 50 amp
Dockside water connections—yes
Waste pump-out—yes
Showers—yes
Laundromat—yes
Gasoline—yes
Diesel fuel—yes
Boat ramp—yes
Ship's store—yes
Restaurant—on site

It's been reported that there are rocks close to the western shore of Lake Michigan north of 59th Street Harbor and possibly not depicted on NOAA chart 14926. It may be a good idea to keep a steady eye on the depthfinder and not creep too closely to that Chicago shore, if you're traveling in between Burnham Park Harbor and 59th Street Harbor Marina. The 59th Street Harbor Marina sits about four miles south of McCormick Place. There is a low, 10-foot clearance bridge before this harbor. Lower than usual water levels may also present entry problems at 59th Street Harbor and the Jackson Park marinas. In the fall of 2000, the Corps of Engineers reported that Lake Michigan was more than a foot lower in 2000 than it was in 1999.

Downtown Chicago skyline off the starboard bow

Our GPS way point outside the 59th Street Harbor Marina is 41.47.31N/87.34.30W. The marina, an unstuffy place, is home to the Museum Shores Yacht Club. For Lake Michigan, this is a relatively small marina, with about 140 slips each capable of accommodating about a 35 footer. There is a seasonal restaurant within walking distance at Jackson Park Outer Marina.

**59th Street Harbor Marina (312) 747-7019;
    VHF 67**

Approach depth—3 feet

**Accepts transients—limited
Floating wooden and steel docks—yes
Dockside power connections—30 amp
Dockside water connections—yes
Restaurant—nearby (seasonal)**

The entrance to the Jackson Park marinas is about a mile southeast of the entrance to 59th Street Harbor Marina. Beware of the long breakwater jutting north of the Jackson Park Harbor entrance. Our GPS way point outside these marinas is 41.46.86N/87.33.92W. There are two marinas inside the channel from this

The Chicago skyline from Lake Michigan

way point. The first one, Jackson Park Outer Harbor Marina, is for sailboats. At the southwest corner of the basin, there is an 11-foot vertical-clearance fixed road bridge. Jackson Park Inner Harbor Marina is a powerboat marina on the other side of this low bridge. Each marina has about 80-90 slips and can accommodate up to 40 footers. The Southern Shores Yacht Club is based in Jackson Park Inner Harbor Marina.

Jackson Park Outer Harbor Marina (312) 747-6189; VHF 67

Approach depth—4-6 feet, but was to be dredged deeper
Accepts transients—limited (advance notification recommended)
Floating wooden piers—yes
Dockside power connections—30 amp
Dockside water connections—yes
Waste pump-out—yes
Showers—yes
Laundromat—yes
Gasoline—yes
Diesel fuel—yes
Ship's store—very limited
Restaurant—on site (seasonal, no breakfast)

Jackson Park Inner Harbor Marina (312) 747-6283; VHF 67

Approach depth—same or less than Jackson Park Outer
Accepts transients—limited (advance notification recommended)
Floating wooden piers—yes
Dockside power connections—30 amp
Dockside water connections—yes
Boat ramp—yes
Restaurant—nearby (seasonal)

A very nice beach, perhaps one of Chicago's nicest, is situated on Lake Michigan a little more than a mile south of the Jackson Park Harbor entry. The large water filtration plant is just southeast of this beach. The plant has its own breakwater. Calumet Harbor is two miles southeast of the plant. Calumet Harbor, like Chicago Harbor, is a large breakwater-protected area extending into Lake Michigan and past the entrance to the Calumet River. There is a nice park with boat launch ramps and a U.S. Coast Guard Station, (773) 768-4093, on the southwest side of Calumet Harbor. The harbor's breakwater, nearly two miles long, has a break in it about halfway out. You may wish to use this pass, if you are entering the Calumet from the north or east (i.e., anywhere but from the Hammond area). Our GPS way point in Lake Michigan just outside this breach in the breakwater is 41.44.24N/87.30.18W.

The Hammond Marina facility is a little more than two miles south of Calumet Harbor. This marina is also the closest one to the entrance of the Calumet River. Hammond Marina is a huge facility with over 1,000 slips, a beach, picnic areas, and a yacht club. There is an inner and outer breakwater wall surrounding nearly all of the marina. Be careful; the outer wall is partially submerged. The entrance through these walls is close to the shore, at the southeast corner of the marina facility. Hammond Marina offers Boat/US discounts. It also has a crane capable of stepping and unstepping sailboat masts. Great Lakes

Inland Marine, (219) 473-1806, across the street, will perform mechanical and below-waterline repairs at Hammond Marina. There is also a casino ship and facility adjacent to the marina.

Hammond Marina (219) 659-7678; VHF 69

Accepts transients—yes
Floating wood piers—yes
Dockside power connections—30 and twin 50 amp
Dockside water connections—yes
Waste pump-out—yes
Showers—yes
Laundromat—yes
Gasoline—yes
Diesel fuel—yes
Mechanical repairs—yes (nearby contractor)
Below-waterline repairs—yes (nearby contractor)
Boat ramp—yes
Ship's store and deli—yes

The next chapter traces the exit from Lake Michigan via the Calumet River. If you are exiting via the Chicago River, skip to chapter 7.

Cranes, tipples, and a conveyor on the Calumet

CHAPTER 6

The Calumet Waterway

The Calumet River enters Lake Michigan at Calumet Harbor at mile 333.5 of the Illinois Waterway System. The Calumet is one of the most industrialized waterways that I've ever sailed. The first seven miles are perhaps even more heavily industrialized than Baltimore's Patapsco River. The Calumet is full of steel-belt manufacturing or the hulks of these industries. We even encountered a large oceangoing freighter trying to nimbly ply its way out of the Calumet River two miles from Lake Michigan.

There are a dozen bridges, street and rail, in this heavily industrialized area. In the late 1980s, one of those oceangoing freighters struck and knocked down a not-quite-fully-opened bascule bridge. The one fixed highway bridge and the "lifted" vertical-lift railway bridges in this area have an unimpeded vertical clearance of no less than 120 feet. All of the railroad bridges are lift, and a few of them are open much of the time. The first, the Elgin, Joliet & Eastern Railroad Lift Bridge, is often open. If not, the clearance is only seven feet.

After this bridge, the lowest closed clearance on the bascule (draw) street bridges is around 18 feet. They should open, if you need more clearance. Nevertheless, you will still be limited by 19 feet of vertical clearance about 30 miles down the river by an un-opening railroad bridge at mile 300.6, after the Calumet connects to the Chicago Sanitary and Ship Canal. The Calumet route generally allows you two feet more of overhead clearance than that found on the Chicago River. On the Chicago River, there are un-opening bridges with only 17 feet of vertical clearance at miles 320.3, 319.9, and 317.6.

Over the Calumet, there are also many fixed overhead cables, pipelines, and conveyors. Extrapolating data from the Corps of Engineers charts, the lowest clearance on these overhead obstructions appears to be no less than 27 feet, and higher than the 24-foot lowest fixed bridge clearances. The following table lists the bridges in this chapter. The bridges of greatest concern are indicated in boldface.

BRIDGE NAME	TYPE	VERTICAL CLEARANCE (FEET)		APPROX RIVER MILE
		CLOSED	UNIMPEDED	
Calumet Harbor, Lake Michigan				333.5
Elgin, Joliet & Eastern Railroad	Lift	7	125	**332.8**
92nd Street	Bascule	18	unlimited	332.6
95th Street	Bascule	23	unlimited	332.3
ConRail Railroad	Lift	120*	120	332.0
ConRail Railroad	Lift	120*	120	332.0
ConRail Railroad	Lift	23	120	332.0
Chicago Skyway	Fixed	125	125	331.9
East 100th Street	Bascule	18**	unlimited	331.6
East 106th Street	Bascule	19**	unlimited	330.8
Indiana Harbor Belt Railroad	Lift	22	125	328.2
South Torrence Avenue	Lift	24	126	328.1
Norfolk Southern Railroad	Lift	24	125	327.7
Confluence at Little Calumet River				327.2
East 130th Street	Fixed	29	**29**	**327.0**
Chicago South Shore Railroad	Fixed	25	**25**	**326.9**
Thomas O'Brien Lock and Dam	Lock			326.4
Conrail Railroad	Fixed	24	**24**	**325.4**
Calumet Expressway	Fixed	39	39	324.6
Indiana Harbor Belt Railroad	Fixed	24	24	322.7
South Indiana Avenue	Fixed	25	25	322.4
Illinois Central Gulf Railroad	Fixed	25	25	322.2
South Halsted Street	Fixed	24	24	320.2
Confluence at Cal-Sag Channel				319.6
Ashland Avenue	Fixed	26	26	319.0
Dan Ryan Expressway	Fixed	41	41	318.9
Division Street	Fixed	24	24	318.5
Chatham Street	Fixed	24	24	318.2
Western Avenue	Fixed	44	44	318.0
Chicago, Rock Island Railroad	Fixed	24	24	317.9
Baltimore & Ohio Railroad	Fixed	24	24	317.6
Grand Trunk Western Railroad	Fixed	24	24	317.6
Grand Trunk Western Railroad	Fixed	24	24	317.5
Baltimore & Ohio Railroad	Fixed	24	24	317.5
Grand Trunk Western Railroad	Fixed	24	24	317.5

BRIDGE NAME	TYPE	VERTICAL CLEARANCE (FEET)		APPROX RIVER MILE
Francisco Avenue	Fixed	24	24	317.3
Kedzie Avenue	Fixed	24	24	316.9
Crawford Avenue	Fixed	26	26	315.9
Northern Illinois Toll Highway	Fixed	39	39	315.6
Cicero Avenue	Fixed	24	24	314.9
127th Street	Fixed	24	24	314.2
Ridgeland Avenue	Fixed	24	24	312.5
Harlem Avenue	Fixed	24	24	311.5
Norfolk & Southern Railroad	Fixed	43	43	310.8
Southwest Highway	Fixed	26	26	310.7
96th Avenue	Fixed	24	24	308.4
104th Avenue	Fixed	24	24	307.4
Sag Highway	Fixed	39	39	304.2
Illinois Central Gulf Railroad	Fixed	24	**24**	**304.0**
Confluence at Chicago Sanitary and Ship Canal				303.5

*Bridge permanently opened
**NOAA chart 14929 indicates *less*—17 feet

A series of lift bridges on the Calumet

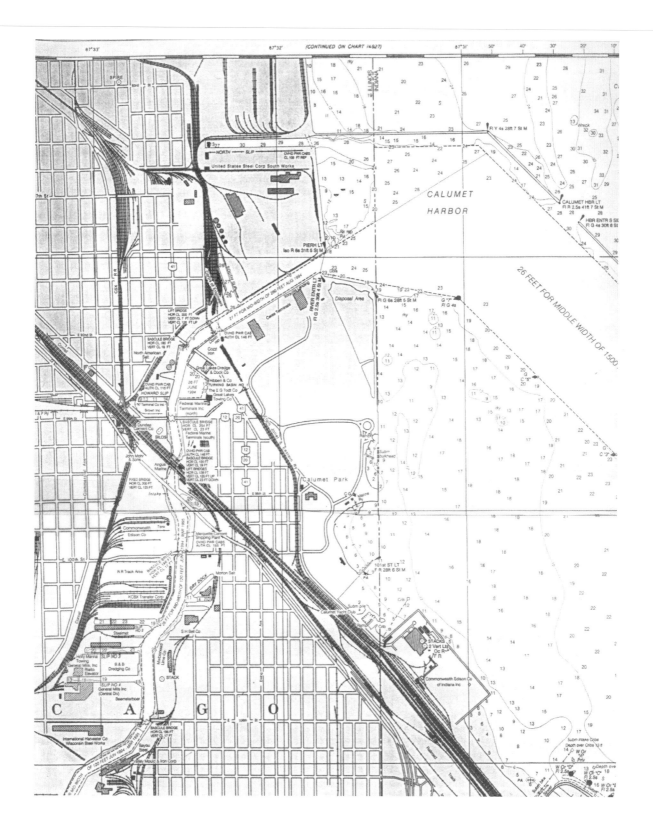

The NOAA chart excerpt here depicts Lake Michigan's Calumet Harbor and some of the Calumet River. There is a turning basin in the river near the western part of the industrial area and near mile 327.2. The river also forks here. The channel to the west extends toward Lake Calumet into an area of more industry. The channel to the south is the Little Calumet River and the direction most of us will head. You will find the Thomas O'Brien Lock and Dam about a half-mile into the Little Calumet River.

The O'Brien Lock is on the west side of the river. The lock tender monitors VHF 16 and will likely switch you to VHF channel 14. The phone number for O'Brien Lock is (773) 646-2183. Near the end of the lockwall, there is also a setup for a recreational vessel to send an audio signal to attract the lock master's attention. Once in the locking pit, a recreational vessel can secure itself by grabbing a rail or other attachment point on the lockwall with a boat hook or line. The drop or lift on the Calumet here is very small at 0-3 feet. The O'Brien Lock, like the lock on the Chicago River, regulates the flow direction of the Calumet River.

After the O'Brien Lock, the Calumet generally flows downhill. From here as far as Cairo, Illinois, or all the way to New Orleans, should you stay on the Mississippi River, the rivers descend. As you descend to Cairo, your right bank is commonly called the RDB, or Right Descending Bank. Your left bank is commonly called the LDB, or Left Descending Bank. By using this well-established standard, two boats, traveling in opposite directions, can ascertain the same meaning. The LDB will always be on your *left* side if you are going *down* the river. If you are going *up* the river, the LDB will always be on your *right* side. We will use this LDB or RDB convention from now on to indicate to which bank we are referring.

There are 11 marinas, most of them small, within seven miles of the O'Brien Lock. See the drawing depicting their locations. Five small marinas are on the LDB (or east) side of the Little Calumet River and within a mile south of the O'Brien Lock. Three of those, Riverside, Sunset Harbor, and Windjammer marinas, are near mile 326, upriver from the un-navigable fork with the Grand Calumet River. Riverside and Windjammer each have about 30 slips and can accommodate to about 50 footers. Sunset Harbor is smaller, and it was for sale. All three marinas have travel lifts as well as repair capabilities. There are restaurants at both Riverside and Windjammer marinas.

Riverside Marina (773) 646-9867

Accepts transients—limited
Fixed wooden docks—yes
Dockside power connections—30 amp
Dockside water connections—yes
Mechanical repairs—limited
Below-waterline repairs—yes
Boat ramp—yes
Restaurant—on site

Sunset Harbor Marina (773) 646-0052

Approach depth—6 feet
Accepts transients—no
Fixed wooden piers—yes
Dockside power connections—15 and 20 amp
Dockside water connections—yes
Mechanical repairs—yes
Below-waterline repairs—yes (10-ton open-ended lift)
Restaurant—several nearby

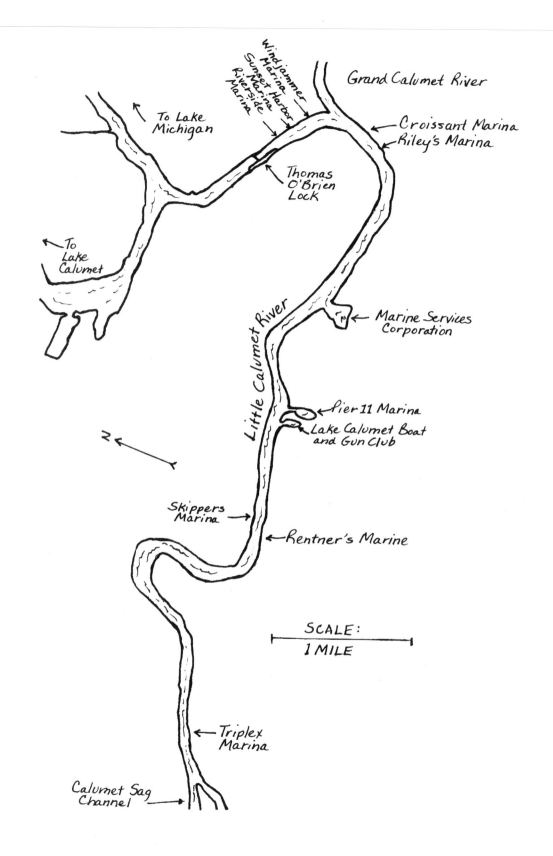

Grand Calumet River

Windjammer Marina
Sunset Harbor Marina
Riverside Marina

Croissant Marina
Riley's Marina

To Lake Michigan

Thomas O'Brien Lock

To Lake Calumet

Little Calumet River

Marine Services Corporation

Pier 11 Marina
Lake Calumet Boat and Gun Club

N

Skippers Marina

Rentner's Marine

SCALE:
1 MILE

Triplex Marina

Calumet Sag Channel

Docks at the Waterfront Pub, on the Calumet

Windjammer Marina (773) 646-2077

Approach depths—3-5 feet
Accepts transients—limited
Fixed steel and floating wooden docks—yes
Dockside power connections—20 amp
Dockside water connections—yes
Below-waterline repairs—yes
Boat ramp—yes
Restaurant—on site

Croissant Marina and Riley's Marina, closer to mile 325 and downriver from the fork with the Grand Calumet River, are on the Little Calumet River. Both marinas have 25-ton open-ended travel lifts for hauling boats, and the capability to perform mechanical repairs. Each has about 40 slips. Croissant can handle up to a 55 footer, and Riley's can handle up to a 15-foot beam. Both marinas house yacht clubs. The Croissant Marina has two restaurants—the Waterfront Pub and the more upscale Croissant Yacht Club Restaurant. Smuggler's Cove Restaurant is next door to Riley's Marina.

Both marinas appear to be well managed.

Croissant Marina (708) 891-0400

Accepts transients—yes
Fixed wooden and steel docks—yes
Dockside power connections—30 amp
Dockside water connections—yes
Showers—yes
Laundromat—yes
Mechanical repairs—yes
Below-waterline repairs—yes
Ship's store—yes
Restaurant—2 on site

Riley's Marina (708) 868-0567

Approach depth—4-5 feet
Accepts transients—limited
Fixed and floating wooden and steel docks—yes
Dockside power connections—30 amp
Dockside water connections—yes
Showers—yes
Mechanical repairs—yes
Below-waterline repairs—yes
Boat ramp—nearby
Restaurant—several nearby

You'll find another five marinas in the next two-mile section of the Little Calumet River. All but one are on the LDB. Marine Services Corporation Marina is about a mile past Riley's Marina on the LDB in a sizable basin off of the river. Marine Services Corporation has a professionally maintained large yard and more yard resources than any other place on the Calumet. The facility also has about 40 slips and can accommodate about a 100 footer.

Marine Services Corporation (708) 841-5660

Approach depth—12 feet
Dockside depth—8 feet
Accepts transients—limited
Floating wooden and steel docks—yes
Dockside power connections—30 amp
Dockside water connections—yes
Waste pump-out—yes
Showers—yes
Mechanical repairs—yes
Below-waterline repairs—yes
Ship's store—yes

Pier 11 Marina and the Lake Calumet Boat and Gun Club are about a mile downstream from Marine Services Corporation and also on the LDB. Pier 11 has some limited river frontage, but the facility is mostly a yard for hauling out large boats with a 50-ton open-ended travel lift. The Lake Calumet Boat and Gun Club is inside a cramped and shallow cut. The club has about 30 slips in a small narrow arm. If your draft is not the limiting factor, a boat to about 30 feet in length could be accommodated. The club's commodore, Chris, wouldn't let us get out of this friendly club without first drinking a beer.

Pier 11 Marina (773) 468-9605

Approach depth—6 feet
Accepts transients—yes
Fixed wooden piers—yes
Dockside power connections—30 and 50 amp

Mechanical repairs—yes
Below-waterline repairs—yes
Ship's store—yes

Lake Calumet Boat and Gun Club (773) 821-9794

Approach depth—4 feet or less
Accepts transients—limited
Fixed wooden piers—yes
Dockside power connections—20 amp
Dockside water connections—yes
Showers—yes
Clubhouse—yes

Skipper's Marina is the only one on the RDB (or north) side and Rentner's Marine is across on the LDB. Both are about a half-mile downriver from Pier 11 Marina. Skipper's is the only marina on the Calumet offering gas, so the fuel dock can be crowded. Skipper's also has a friendly lounge and a very nice picnic area. Both Skipper's and Rentner's have fewer than 10 slips, and both can accommodate 30 footers. Rentner's Marine has a neat and well-maintained yard, but it limits transients due to space constraints.

Skipper's Marina (708) 841-1300

Accepts transients—yes
Fixed wooden piers—yes
Waste pump-out—yes
Showers—yes
Gasoline—yes
Mechanical repairs—limited
Below-waterline repairs—limited (with a forklift)
Boat ramp—yes
Ship's store—very limited
Lounge—yes

Rentner's Marine (773) 468-3776

Accepts transients—very limited
Fixed steel docks—yes
Dockside power connections—20 amp
Dockside water connections—yes
Mechanical repairs—yes
Below-waterline repairs—yes
Ship's store—yes

Captain Rick and *Free State* at the Worth Municipal Boat Launch

Triplex Marina is about two and a half miles past Rentner's and also on the LDB. It is the last marina on the Calumet; the next bona-fide marina is 42 miles downriver and on the Des Plaines River. Triplex Marina has a well-stocked ship's store. The marina has about 50 slips and about 100 feet of river frontage on a floodwall. There is also a 50-ton open-ended lift for haul-outs. Larry has been doing the work here for 30 years.

Triplex Marina (708) 849-2200

Approach depth—12 feet
Dockside depth—5-12 feet
Accepts transients—yes
Fixed wooden and steel docks—yes
Dockside power connections—30 amp
Dockside water connections—yes
Mechanical repairs—yes
Below-waterline repairs—yes
Boat ramp—yes
Ship's store—yes
Restaurant—on site

Your main Calumet channel becomes the Cal-Sag Channel, as the Little Calumet River fades into a creek on the LDB side about a half-mile west of Triplex Marina. You'll see a large weather dome to the southwest side (LDB) of the Cicero Avenue Bridge, five miles past Triplex Marina.

About a mile and a half past Cicero Avenue, you'll come to the first of two ramp areas with nice docks. Both are on the RDB (north) side of the Cal-Sag Channel. There is a pleasing small water park, Howie's Landing, on the RDB of the Cal-Sag about two miles past that first ramp area. The Worth Municipal Boat Launch area is about a half-mile west of Howie's Landing. The Cal-Sag Channel has now become a tasteful waterway. It will continue to be a modestly nice waterway until it intersects with the Chicago Sanitary and Ship Canal another eight miles to the west. In my opinion, the 12-mile westernmost stretch of the Cal-Sag is a much more eye- and nose-pleasing route than the alternative corresponding route on the Chicago Sanitary and Ship Canal.

Skyscrapers along the Chicago River

CHAPTER 7

The Chicago River and Chicago Sanitary and Ship Canal

The Chicago River runs through the heart of downtown Chicago and the Loop. This short river, with its North Branch and South Branch, once flowed into Lake Michigan. With the construction of the Illinois Waterway, the flow of the Chicago River was reversed. The primary purpose of the Chicago River Lock is to regulate that change to "mother nature" and to facilitate the maintenance of the navigable waterway for commercial and recreational boats. After the Chicago River Lock, the river flows downhill toward the heart of Illinois. As you go farther from Lake Michigan on the Chicago River, your right bank is commonly called the RDB, or Right Descending Bank. Your left bank is commonly called the LDB, or Left Descending Bank. This is a well-established standard. The RDB will always be on your *right* side if you are going *downriver.* If you are going *up* the river, the RDB will always be on your *left* side.

The large and commercially developed Navy Pier sits about a quarter-mile north of the Chicago River entrance. Dime Pier is the partially exposed pier south of the Navy Pier. Dime Pier is an old wooden pier that got its name long ago when boats would charge a dime to take fishermen out to this pier for the day. Our way point out on Lake Michigan and near the Chicago River entry is 41.53.29N/87.35.36W. This is outside the last breakwater for Chicago Harbor and near a gap in the breakwater wall. We also have another way point, inside the breakwater but before the Chicago River—41.53.29N/87.35.70W. The NOAA chart excerpt here depicts this area well. A significant portion of the South Branch of the Chicago River in downtown Chicago is depicted on the next NOAA chart excerpt. Both excerpts are taken from NOAA chart 14928.

As you near the Chicago River Lock, leave both the Navy Pier and Dime Pier to your north. There is no dam at this lock. The water level difference between Lake Michigan and the Chicago River is between 0 and 3 feet. The Chicago River Lock monitors VHF 16 and then they'll likely switch you to VHF 14. The lock can also be reached at phone (312) 787-4795. The Chicago Police Marine Unit is located just inside the Chicago River Lock. This unit monitors VHF 16 and can be reached at phone (312) 744-4817. The water to the north, just after the Chicago River Lock, leads to a narrow channel heading west for about a half-mile. This area is known as Ogden Slip. Ogden Slip houses a few upscale restaurants and some private condominiums.

There is a nice pedestrian river walk on the LDB (i.e., south) side of the Chicago River. This is reminiscent of Fort Lauderdale, Florida, with all of the urbanization on a city waterway. But you need to keep "your eyes on the water" and pay close attention. There are many overhead bridges too—Lake Shore Drive, Columbus Avenue, and Michigan Avenue. Many tour boats tie up on both sides of the Chicago River west of the Michigan Avenue Bridge.

After a downtown bridge opens and re-closes, a roving team of bridge tenders runs from that bridge to another bridge, perhaps two or three bridges away "down the route."

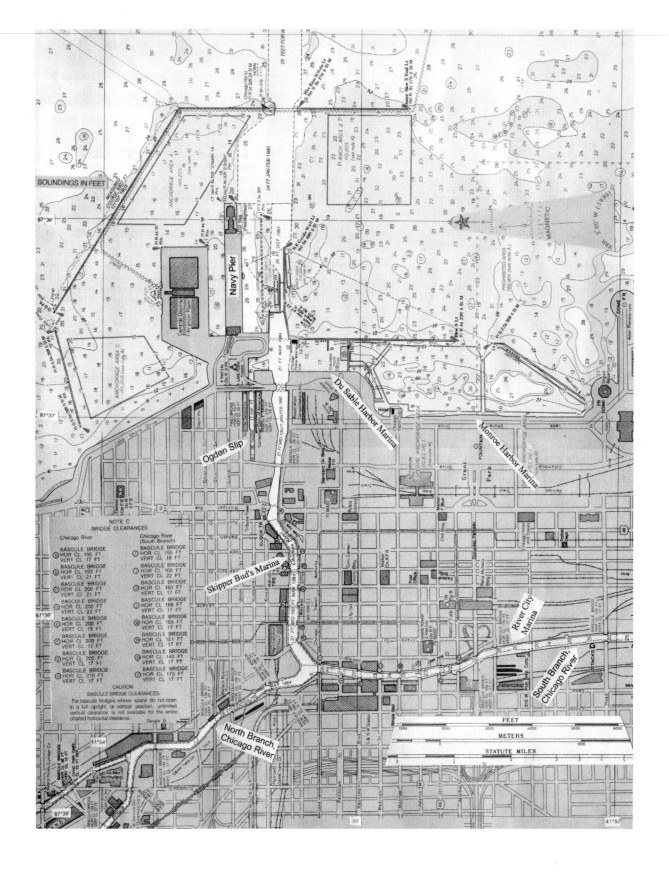

SOUNDINGS IN FEET

Navy Pier

Ogden Slip

Du Sable Harbor Marina

Monroe Harbor Marina

Skipper Bud's Marina

River City Marina

South Branch, Chicago River

North Branch, Chicago River

NOTE C
BRIDGE CLEARANCES

Chicago River	Chicago River (South Branch)
BASCULE BRIDGE HOR CL 195 FT VERT CL 17 FT	BASCULE BRIDGE HOR CL 195 FT VERT CL 18 FT
BASCULE BRIDGE HOR CL 193 FT VERT CL 21 FT	BASCULE BRIDGE HOR CL 100 FT VERT CL 22 FT
BASCULE BRIDGE HOR CL 200 FT VERT CL 21 FT	BASCULE BRIDGE HOR CL 160 FT VERT CL 17 FT
BASCULE BRIDGE HOR CL 200 FT VERT CL 22 FT	BASCULE BRIDGE HOR CL 168 FT VERT CL 17 FT
BASCULE BRIDGE HOR CL 200 FT VERT CL 19 FT	BASCULE BRIDGE HOR CL 185 FT VERT CL 17 FT
BASCULE BRIDGE HOR CL 200 FT VERT CL 17 FT	BASCULE BRIDGE HOR CL 151 FT VERT CL 17 FT
BASCULE BRIDGE HOR CL 200 FT VERT CL 17 FT	BASCULE BRIDGE HOR CL 140 FT VERT CL 17 FT
BASCULE BRIDGE HOR CL 210 FT VERT CL 17 FT	BASCULE BRIDGE HOR CL 170 FT VERT CL 17 FT

CAUTION
BASCULE BRIDGE CLEARANCES
For bascule bridges whose spans do not open
to a full upright or vertical position, unlimited
vertical clearance is not available for the entire
charted horizontal clearance.

FEET

METERS

STATUTE MILES

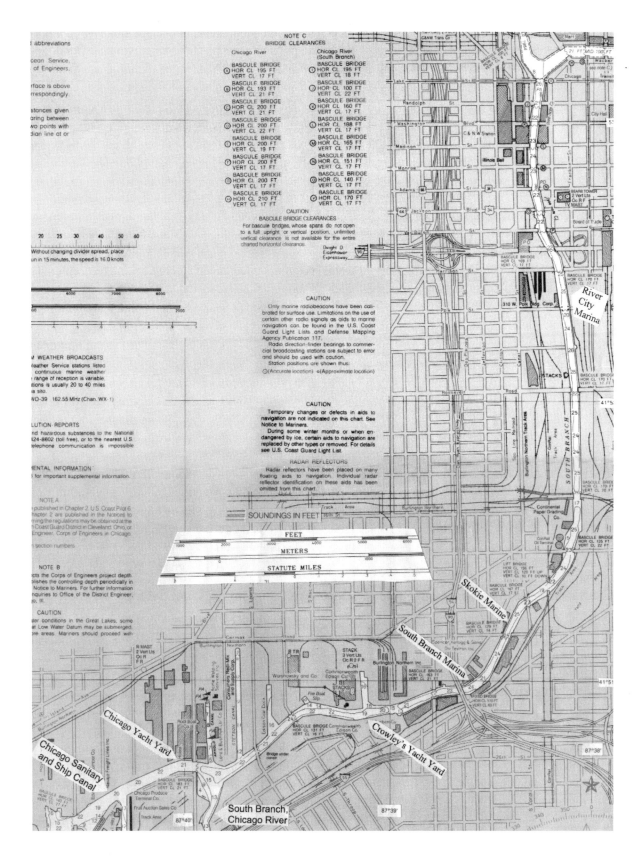

BRIDGE NAME	TYPE	VERTICAL CLEARANCE (FEET)		APPROX RIVER MILE
		CLOSED	UNIMPEDED	
Chicago River Lock	Lock			327.2
Lake Shore Drive	Bascule	25	unlimited	326.9
Columbus AvenueBascule		21	unlimited	326.6
Michigan Avenue	Bascule	17	unlimited	326.4
Wabash Avenue	Bascule	22 (fn. 1)	unlimited	326.3
State Street	Bascule	21	unlimited	326.2
Dearborn Street	Bascule	22	unlimited	326.1
Clark Street	Bascule	19	unlimited	326.0
La Salle Street	Bascule	18 (fn. 2)	unlimited	325.9
Wells Street	Bascule	18 (fn. 2)	unlimited	325.8
Franklin-Orleans Street	Bascule	18 (fn. 2)	unlimited	325.7
Confluence at South Branch				325.6
Lake Street	Bascule	18	unlimited	325.6
Randolph Street	Bascule	22 (fn. 3)	unlimited	325.5
Washington Street	Bascule	20 (fn. 2)	unlimited	325.4
Madison Street	Bascule	18 (fn. 2)	unlimited	325.3
Monroe Street	Bascule	18 (fn. 2)	unlimited	325.2
Adams Street	Bascule	19 (fn. 2)	unlimited	325.1
Jackson Boulevard	Bascule	20 (fn. 2)	unlimited	325.0
Van Buren Street	Bascule	22 (fn. 2)	unlimited	324.9
Eisenhower Expressway	Bascule	22 (fn. 2)	unlimited	324.8
Harrison Street	Bascule	22 (fn. 2)	unlimited	324.7
Roosevelt Road	Bascule	16 (fn. 4)	unlimited	324.3
Baltimore & Ohio Railroad	Bascule	21 (fn. 5)	unlimited	323.9
Conrail Railroad	Bascule	22 (fn. 5)	unlimited	323.8
18th Street	Bascule	22	unlimited	323.7
Amtrak Railroad	Lift	**10**	65	**323.5**
Canal Street	Bascule	22 (fn. 2)	unlimited	323.4
Cermak Road	Bascule	**14** (fn. 6)	unlimited	**323.3**
Dan Ryan Expressway	Fixed	63	63	322.9
South Halsted Street	Bascule	21	unlimited	322.8
South Loomis Street	Bascule	22 (fn. 7)	unlimited	321.9
Confluence at Chicago S&S Canal				321.7
South Ashland Avenue	Bascule	21	unlimited	321.6

BRIDGE NAME	TYPE	VERTICAL CLEARANCE (FEET)		APPROX RIVER MILE
		CLOSED	UNIMPEDED	
South Damen Avenue	Bascule	27	unlimited	321.1
South Western Avenue	Fixed	22	22	320.5
B&O Railroad	Bascule	17	**17***	**320.3**
South California Avenue	Bascule	17	**17***	**319.9**
Illinois Central Gulf Railroad	Swing	19	19*	319.5
South Kedzie Avenue	Fixed	22	22	319.4
Grand Trunk Western Railroad	Swing	18	18*	318.9
South Pulaski Road	Bascule	22	22*	318.4
Belt Railroad	Swing	17	**17***	**317.6**
South Cicero Avenue	Bascule	18	18*	317.3
South Central Avenue	Fixed	42	42	316.2
A., Topeka & Santa Fe Railroad	Swing	18	18*	314.8
South Harlem Avenue	Bascule	23	23*	314.0
Adlai Stevenson Expressway	Fixed	41	41	313.4
Lawndale Avenue	Fixed	39	39	313.0
B&O Railroad	Swing	18	18*	312.2
Mannheim (La Grange) Road	Fixed	39	39	309.3
Northern Illinois Expressway	Fixed	39	39	309.1
Willow Springs Road	Fixed	18 (fn. 8)	18	307.9
Sag Highway	Fixed	39	39	304.1
Confluence with Calumet channel				303.5

Bridge Clearance Discrepancies (fn.):
>   (fn. 1) NOAA chart 14928 indicates *less*—21 feet
>   (fn. 2) NOAA chart 14928 indicates *less*—17 feet
>   (fn. 3) Corps of Engineers chart indicates *less*—17 feet
>   (fn. 4) Corps of Engineers chart indicates more—25 feet
>   (fn. 5) NOAA chart 14928 indicates *less*—20 feet
>   (fn. 6) superintendent of bridges stated more—16 feet
>   (fn. 7) Corps of Engineers chart indicates *less*—13 feet
>   (fn. 8) *U.S. Coast Pilot* indicates a 39-foot bascule bridge

*Bridge does not open for navigation

Chicago River bridge tenders monitor VHF channel 12. And there are also several telephone numbers for these bridges: (a) the bridge lift coordinator at (312) 744-8700; (b) the superintendent of bridges at (312) 745-3112 or (312) 745-3113; (c) the Lake Shore Drive Bridge, from 7:00 A.M. to 3:00 P.M., at (312) 744-4280; or (d) the 24-hour telephone number at (312) 744-4200. Another telephone number that may be able to help you with bridge clearances as well as water depth is the local Corps of Engineers Office at (312) 353-6400.

If you require less than 16 feet of clearance, you should be able to make it under all unopened downtown bridges at normal pool level stage, except for two. Beware—the Conrail/ Amtrak railroad lift bridge is about three miles farther up the river with only about 10 feet of vertical clearance when the lift span is in the closed position. The Cermak Road Bridge is a fifth of a mile past the Amtrak Bridge, and this bridge only has 14 feet of vertical clearance when closed. After Cermak Road, and in the Chicago Sanitary and Ship Canal, there are three bridges with only 17 feet of overhead clearance, and these bridges no longer open. If you need between 17 and 19 feet of overhead clearance, the Calumet Waterway is your only route south. The previous table lists the bridges in this chapter before the confluence with the Calumet. There is another table for those bridges after the confluence with the Cal-Sag (i.e., the Calumet) waterway.

The Wabash Avenue Bridge and Sun Times Building on the Chicago

The old Marina City Marina is now Skipper Bud's Marina, on the RDB (north) side after the State Street Bridge. Skipper Bud's has a very limited number of small private slips and nothing available for recreational transient boaters. But there is a restaurant, (312) 629-2976, across the river that welcomes dining boaters.

Skipper Bud's Marina (847) 872-3200

Accepts transients—no
Mechanical repairs—yes
Restaurant—across the river

After Skipper Bud's, you'll go under Dearborn, Clark, La Salle, Wells, and Franklin-Orleans streets. After the Franklin-Orleans Bridge, there is a sizable fork in the river. The fork on the RDB is the North Branch of the Chicago River. If you took this fork for about 17 miles, you would reach the Wilmette Lock back on Lake Michigan. But the Wilmette Lock is inoperable and there is no access to the lake. On this North Branch route, you'd go under eight drawbridges before coming to the first of many fixed and a few more opening bridges. The lowest of these many fixed bridges have about 17 feet of vertical clearance at the normal pool level. The Corps of Engineers ends the maintained navigable channel about six miles from this Chicago River fork, at the Addison Street Bridge. It's about another 11 miles to the Wilmette Lock and Evanston, Illinois. According to NOAA chart 14926, there is no channel depth of less than seven feet, except near where this North Shore channel nears Lake Michigan. Near the lake, the NOAA chart indicates areas as shallow as three feet.

At that North Branch fork, nearly all of us will be bearing left, or south toward the LDB

onto the South Branch of the Chicago River. We are in the heart of downtown Chicago, still pressed in by the skyscraper canyon. We will go beneath Lake, Randolph, Washington, and Madison streets. We'll see the Civic Opera House on our left. The Sears Tower, one of the tallest buildings in the world, is only two blocks to our southeast.

In this manmade city canyon, we'll go under Monroe Street, Adams Street, and Jackson Boulevard. There is a water taxi service between Adams Street and Jackson Boulevard. On the west side, the RDB, there are a few waterside restaurants.

Van Buren Street, Eisenhower Expressway, and Harrison Street follow. The urban canyon starts thinning out after Van Buren Street. After the expressway, the shore is a bit more park-like. The River City Marina complex is after Harrison Street but before Roosevelt Road on the LDB (east) side. It is a fancy condominium complex with about 60 slips, but none are available for transient boaters.

River City Marina (312) 431-2800

Accepts transients—no
Floating wooden piers—yes
Dockside power connections—30 and 50 amp
Dockside water connections—yes
Waste pump-out—yes
Laundromat—yes
Restaurant—several nearby

After River City Marina, there will be more bridges and a few of them are railroad bridges. The Amtrak station is on the RDB side. You really have to watch your noggin at the second railroad bridge near mile 323.5. Unopened, the vertical clearance of this bridge is only around 10 feet. The three marinas downriver have repaired more than a few broken flying bridges on boats. Be careful here. Radio VHF 16 or telephone (312) 930-4125 beforehand to ask for an opening. After that railroad bridge, you'll find Skokie Marine and South Branch Marina on the RDB side. Skokie Marine operates an on-the-water towing service and asserts that mechanical repairs are their forte. They can accommodate about 20 side-tied boats. South Branch Marina has room for about 10 side-tied boats on the Chicago River. Both marinas can haul boats. Skokie has a 20-ton lift, and South Branch has a 15,000-pound forklift truck.

Skokie Marine (847) 679-0300

Approach depth—10 feet
Accepts transients—yes
Floating concrete and steel docks—yes
Dockside power connections—15 and 30 amp
Dockside water connections—yes

Showers—yes
Mechanical repairs—yes
Below-waterline repairs—yes
Ship's store—yes

South Branch Marina (312) 226-0700

Accepts transients—yes
Fixed wooden piers—yes
Dockside power connections—15 amp
Dockside water connections—yes
Waste pump-out—yes
Gasoline—yes
Mechanical repairs—yes
Below-waterline repairs—limited
Ship's store—limited
Café—yes (outdoor)

After South Branch Marina, you'll go under your first fixed bridge, the Dan Ryan Expressway, which has a vertical clearance of 63 feet. The South Branch of the Chicago

The Sears Tower, dead astern on the Chicago River

Crowley's Yacht Yard

River will also turn west here. Crowley's Yacht Yard is less than a half-mile past the Dan Ryan on the LDB shore.

In the Chicago area, and especially on the Chicago River, Crowley's Yacht Yard is a good place to unstep or step sailboat masts. For other mast unstepping alternatives, Hammond Marina as well as a few marinas on the lower eastern shore of Lake Michigan (i.e., in Benton Harbor and Holland, Michigan) can also do this work. If you wish to unstep your sailboat mast on the western shore of Lake Michigan, Crowley's also has a mobile crane that makes occasional trips to the mouth of the Chicago River for mast unstepping purposes. Sailboat masts can be unstepped at Crowley's, and arrangements can be made to transport them to Kentucky Lake, Mobile, Alabama, or other places on the Gulf of Mexico. At normal pool level, the lowest fixed bridge clearances on the

Tennessee River, and on the subsequent Tenn-Tom Waterway, are stated at 52 feet.

Sailboat flotillas are often organized to synchronize travel beneath the more than two dozen heavily used vehicular bridges between Lake Michigan and Crowley's. The Chicago River bridges near downtown will sequentially open for an organized flotilla, but not for the solo sailboat. During the busy season (September to mid-November) there may be two to six of these "bridge-opening" sailboat flotillas per week on the Chicago River.

Crowley's bread and butter is seasonal land storage for local Chicago-area boaters. According to Bruce Rosenzweig, the busy times at Crowley's are October (for boat hauling and unstepping) and May (for stepping and launching). Crowley's may haul or launch around 800 local boats during these busy periods. Hence, transient boaters will likely get better attention at other times. Crowley's has about 1,000 feet of dock frontage on the Chicago River.

Crowley's Yacht Yard (312) 225-2170
http://www.crowleys.com

Approach depth—10 feet
Fixed steel docks—yes
Dockside power connections—limited
Mechanical repairs—yes
Below-waterline repairs—yes
Ship's store—yes (well stocked)
Restaurant—2 nearby

The Chicago Yacht Yard is about a mile downriver from Crowley's, just beyond the Ashland Avenue Bridge on the RDB. Like Crowley's, it is a storage facility, but much smaller. The Chicago Yacht Yard has no short-term haul-outs but could haul a 70-foot sailboat or a 63-foot powerboat with its cranes for long-term storage. Their forte is fiberglass work.

Chicago Yacht Yard (312) 666-6670

Mechanical repairs—yes
Below-waterline repairs—yes

The Chicago Sanitary and Ship Canal becomes our main channel heading southwest less than a mile west of Crowley's Yacht Yard. Here the South Branch of the Chicago River turns southeast. After the initial downtown canyon, the ambiance of the Chicago River fades and you might as well just make time through this portion of waterway. The lowest bridge on the Chicago Sanitary and Ship Canal is a railroad bridge at mile 320.3. This bridge's clearance is 17 feet unopened, and this once-opening bridge no longer opens. Your boat needs 17 feet of clearance or less for this bridge and for a few of the other low bridges downriver on the Chicago Sanitary and Ship Canal. Westward, the canal becomes rather bland with only an industrial flavor. One boat ramp was observed beneath the Archer Avenue Bridge, near mile 313.1 on the LDB. This is a private ramp and a rather steep one. A sprawling water-treatment plant is farther downriver on the RDB. The un-navigable Des Plaines River starts paralleling our canal and it is usually out of sight but less than a quarter of a mile to the north. The Des Plaines River originates in southeastern Wisconsin near Kenosha.

After the Junction with the Cal-Sag Channel

The Calumet, or Cal-Sag Channel, intersects the Chicago Sanitary and Ship Canal at mile 303.5. The Calumet also enters Lake Michigan at Calumet Harbor after a trip of 30 miles (see chapter 6). It's about a seven-mile-shorter route to Lake Michigan on the Chicago Sanitary and Ship Canal, although the bridge clearances are lower than on the Calumet route. Our GPS reading at the junction of the Chicago Sanitary and Ship Canal and the Cal-Sag Channel is 41.41.81N/87.56.95W. There is even a small lighthouse on the point of land separating these two canals.

The southwestward continuation after the junction with the Cal-Sag is still called the Chicago Sanitary and Ship Canal. After the junction with the Calumet, there is a large spread-out staging area for barges. And the river does seem to choke a bit. This area, and until the Lockport Lock, has also not-so-affectionately been called "the twelve miles of hell," because of all of the parked and moving barges, especially between miles 303 to 296.

Another problem that we encountered in our small vessel was the refractive waves. Wakes from barges and larger recreational vessels would bounce off the channel walls and sometimes combine with the initial wake to create very confused seas. These steep, choppy, and confused seas along with the narrow unfriendly shoreline made our navigation through this section most taxing. Extra precaution is advised in this area. Furthermore, there is no means to get "out of the way" (e.g., ramp, dock, or any place to anchor) in this area until after the Lockport Lock and Dam. In my opinion, this section of the lower Chicago Sanitary and Ship Canal is one that you just want to get through without lingering. But remain alert for the barge and recreational vessel traffic.

Furthermore, three miles downriver from the junction with the Cal-Sag there is another railroad bridge that does not open. The vertical clearance of this bridge at mile 300.6 is only 19 feet. If you choose the "higher clearances" on the Cal-Sag route from Lake Michigan, this un-opening swing bridge is your lowest clearance. It also limits towboat operations. Many barges have to switch tows here, because some towboats are too high to negotiate beneath this bridge. The following table lists the bridges between the confluence with the Calumet and the beginning of the Des Plaines River.

BRIDGE NAME	TYPE	VERTICAL CLEARANCE (FEET)		APPROX RIVER MILE
		CLOSED	UNIMPEDED	
Confluence with Calumet Channel				303.5
Illinois Central Gulf Railroad	Swing	**19**	**19***	300.6
Lemont Highway	Fixed	47	47	300.5
135th Street	Fixed	48 **	48	296.2
Route 7 (9th Street Bridge) Lockport	Fixed	47	47	292.7
Lockport Lock	Lock			291.0
Confluence with Des Plaines River				290.0

*Bridge does not open for navigation
**Corps of Engineers chart indicates *less*—a 17-foot swing bridge

The Lockport Dam is on the RDB, and the lock is on the LDB (east) side of the canal. The lock master monitors VHF 16 and 14 and can be reached at phone (815) 838-0536. The lock master will throw two lines from the lockwall to your vessel. The lock can drop or lift over 40 feet. You'll need to adjust the slack in these two lines as your vessel is rising or lowering in the lock pit. And when the water is at the low level, you'll really feel as if you're in the depths of a pit here.

Bicentennial Park on the west bank in Joliet, Illinois

CHAPTER 8

The Des Plaines and Upper Illinois Rivers, from Joliet to Seneca

About a mile south of the Lockport Lock and Dam, the Chicago Sanitary and Ship Canal ends. The once un-navigable Des Plaines River, which has been paralleling to our northwest (i.e., on our RDB side) for the past 24 miles, merges and thankfully takes over. Finally, at mile 290 our waterway becomes an authentic river, and it is no longer an industrial canal. And now we are really going downhill. The river here will likely add about two to three miles per hour to our boat speed. The drawing here depicts the Des Plaines, Kankakee, and Illinois rivers and the 40-mile section of navigable waterway covered in this chapter.

Joliet, Illinois is a great reprieve after that "twelve miles of hell." As you are approaching Joliet, there is a boat ramp on the RDB at mile 288.8. In charming downtown Joliet, there are six bridges; five are bascule street bridges with a vertical clearance of only around 16 feet in the closed position. If the railroad lift bridge isn't in the open position, the vertical clearance is only about nine feet. Several collisions have occurred beneath this bridge. Please use extreme caution here. The Interstate 80 fixed bridge is at the south end of Joliet. The lock tender at the downriver Brandon Road Lock and Dam told me that the Des Plaines water pool level around Joliet doesn't fluctuate much. Joliet is in a section of river that is only about five miles between locks and dams. The following table lists the bridges, locks, and major river confluences covered in this chapter.

Leaving the Lockport Lock on the Des Plaines River

BRIDGE NAME	TYPE	VERTICAL CLEARANCE (FEET)*		APPROX RIVER MILE
		CLOSED	UNIMPEDED	
Confluence with Des Plaines River				290.0
Lockport, Elgin, Joliet Railroad	Lift	24	51	290.0
Ruby Street, Joliet	Bascule	16	47	288.7
Jackson Street, Joliet	Bascule	16	47	288.4
Cass Street, Joliet	Bascule	16	47	288.1
Jefferson Street, Joliet	Bascule	16	47	287.9
Joliet-Chicago Rock Island Railroad	Lift	**9**	50	**287.6**
U.S. Route 6 (McDonough Street), Joliet	Bascule	16	47	287.3
Interstate 80	Fixed	46	46	286.9
Brandon Road Lock and Dam	Lock			286.0
Rockdale-Brandon Road	Bascule	**15****	66	**285.8**
Interstate 55	Fixed	47	47	277.8
Confluence with Kankakee River				272.8
Dresden Island Lock and Dam	Lock			271.5
Elgin, Joliet, & Eastern Railroad	Lift	26	56	270.6
Route 47, Morris	Fixed	50	50	263.5
Chessie System Railroad	Lift	21	47	254.1
Route 170, Seneca	Fixed	47	47	252.7

*Clearance is for normal pool; high water, according to the *U.S. Coast Pilot,* could be 2-18 feet above normal pool

***U.S. Coast Pilot* indicates only an 8-foot "high water" clearance

Between the Cass Street and Jefferson Street bridges, you'll see Harrah's Casino on the LDB. Bicentennial Park is across the river from the casino. This area is near the center of Joliet.

The dockside floodwall at Bicentennial Park is over 300 yards long and there is plenty of room for many side-tied boats. There are no real marinas in Joliet, but you can tie up gratis and possibly even plug into electricity at this park. If you decide to tie up

to the wall overnight, you must leave an anchor light on. Your anchor light alerts the frequent barge traffic to your presence, so the tows can give the floodwall a wider berth. I have heard of an unplanned tow-boat-recreational vessel encounter around Joliet. The larger steel towboat barely got scratched, but the recreational boat was badly mangled. If you tie up in Joliet, please first inquire at the visitor's center building adjacent to the park to obtain the latest

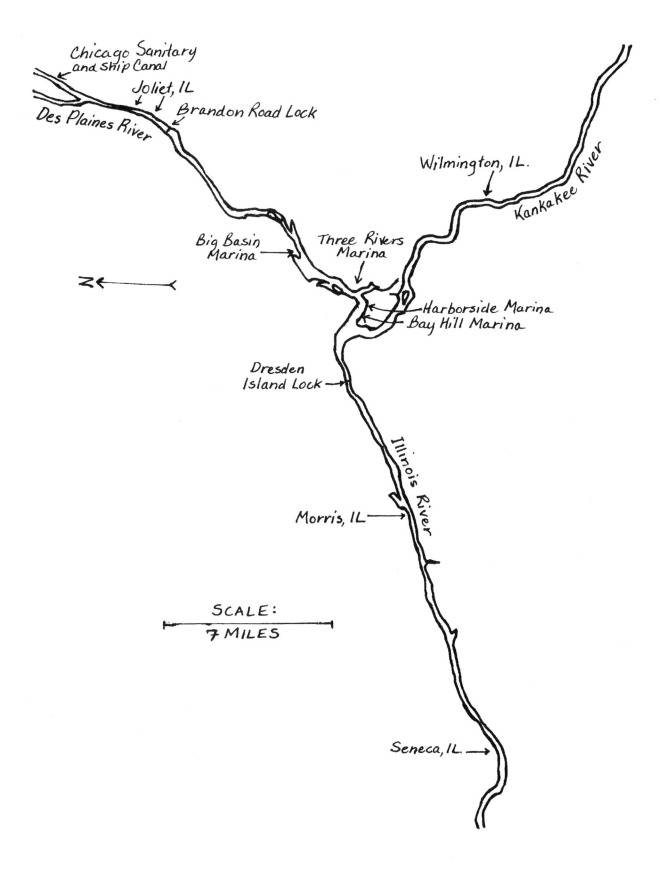

Bicentennial Park regulations. The ambiance at the park is very pleasant, but there are no showers nor bathrooms. If you are here in July, don't miss the fabled "Waterway Days."

Joliet is a nice, clean, manicured city. Most of the nearby restaurants and services are on the east side (LDB) of the Des Plaines River. You will have to walk a bit to the nearest grocery and hardware store; both are northeast of the central business district by about five blocks. There is a historical society museum at the corner of Cass and Ottawa streets. There are a few other hotels, besides Harrah's Casino, in Joliet. The least expensive may be the Hotel Plaza for about $35 (no credit cards). It is downtown, two blocks east of Harrah's. Joliet was founded by Louis Joliet sometime after his great adventure with Marquette. By land, Joliet is the first major stop past Chicago on U.S. Route 66, the historic highway between Chicago and Los Angeles.

There is a sandwich shop with a side-tie docking area on the RDB about a half-mile upriver from the Brandon Road Lock and Dam. This lock and dam is about a mile south of the 46-foot-clearance interstate highway bridge at the south end of Joliet. The lock gates are also on the RDB, while the dam is on the LDB. The lock master prefers VHF 14 but also monitors VHF 16. The lock can also be reached at phone (815) 774-1714. Like at the Lockport Lock, and all locks on the Illinois River, the Brandon Road lock master will throw a couple of lines to your boat from the walls above the pit. When you are locking up, there is slightly more turbulence in the rear of the lock. When you are locking down, the turbulence is uniform and minimal. The lift or drop here is about 34 feet.

There is another casino boat area on the RDB about three miles downriver from the Brandon Road Lock, near mile 283.2. Then you'll go under another high fixed interstate bridge, Interstate 55, at mile 277.8. There is a small commercial boat dock northeast of this bridge on the RDB. Big Basin Marina is on the opposite side of the bridge and also on the RDB. Big Basin Marina has about 120 slips and can accommodate up to a 50 footer. The marina can haul out modest-sized boats with a lift pulled by a truck tractor.

Big Basin Marina (815) 467-2181

Approach depth—5 feet
Accepts transients—yes
Fixed and floating steel docks—yes
Dockside power connections—30 amp
Dockside water connections—yes
Showers—yes
Laundromat—yes
Gasoline—yes
Mechanical repairs—through local contractors
Below-waterline repairs—yes, somewhat limited
Boat ramp—yes
Lounge—serving sandwiches and pizza

Three Rivers Marina is on the LDB at mile 274.9, three miles downriver from Big Basin Marina. The marina has around a 100 slips and can accommodate a 50 to 60 footer depending on the vessel's draft. Three Rivers Marina has two travel lifts, with the larger one being 35 tons and open ended. Boatyard space is ample. The Three Rivers Yacht Club is also housed at this marina.

Three Rivers Marina (815) 476-2324

Approach depth—3-5 feet
Accepts transients—yes
Fixed wooden piers—yes
Dockside power connections—30 amp
Dockside water connections—yes
Showers—yes
Mechanical repairs—yes
Below-waterline repairs—yes
Boat ramp—yes
Ship's store—yes (limited)

Harborside Marina and Bay Hill Marina are about a mile downriver from Three Rivers Marina and also on the LDB. Both are modern, professionally run, well-maintained facilities. Harborside is the first place where a boater can purchase diesel fuel outside of Chicago. Harborside has two basins and can accommodate about 160 vessels up to 100 feet. This first-class marina complex also has a 35-ton travel lift, a forklift, and a swimming pool. Bay Hill Marina is the pier west and next door to Harborside. Bay Hill is primarily a sales/service/indoor-storage facility with a 25-ton travel lift.

Harborside Marina (815) 476-4400
http://www.harborsidemarina.com

Approach depth—6 feet
Accepts transients—yes
Fixed and floating wooden, concrete, and steel
    docks—yes
Dockside power connections—30 and 50 amp
Dockside water connections—yes
Waste pump-out—yes
Showers—yes
Gasoline—yes
Diesel fuel—yes
Mechanical repairs—yes
Below-waterline repairs—yes
Boat ramp—yes

Ship's store—yes
Restaurant—on site

Bay Hill Marina (815) 476-9988
http://www.bayhillmarina.com

Accepts transients—no
Fixed steel dock—yes
Dockside power connections—15 and 30 amp
Mechanical repairs—yes
Below-waterline repairs—yes
Ship's store—yes
Restaurant—nearby

The Kankakee River, entering from the LDB, joins the Des Plaines River less than a mile downriver from Bay Hill Marina. We've been told that there is a fair amount of recreational boating on the sparkling Kankakee. It generally flows from the east from Indiana. At the junction of the Kankakee and Des Plaines rivers, near GPS way point 41.23.63N/88.15.42W, the official head of the Illinois River begins. The Illinois (including the Kankakee and Des Plaines tributaries) drains about one-third of the state, in a swath from the northeast to the southwest. The river and state owe their name to a Native American confederation of Indians known as the Illini. Illiniwek is the plural name these Native Americans gave themselves. The French translated the named as Illinois. And we, in turn, likely corrupted the French pronunciation. The Illini Confederation consisted of five nations: The Kaskaskia, Cahokia, Peoria, Michegamea, and Tamaroa Indians. The archenemy of the Illiniwek were the Iroquois. On this trip south, we'll go past Peoria, and later Cahokia and Kaskaskia, the latter two on the Mississippi River.

The Dresden Nuclear Power Plant is about

a half-mile downriver from the Kankakee River on the LDB of the Illinois River. You can't miss it. The Dresden Island Lock and Dam is about a mile downriver from the nuclear plant. The lock is on the LDB while the dam is on the RDB. The lock master monitors VHF channels 16 and 14 and can be reached at phone (815) 942-0840. The drop or lift at this lock is about 22 feet.

The friendly town of Morris, Illinois is eight miles downriver from the Dresden Island Lock, on the RDB. There is a nice boat ramp with about a 50-foot dock just north of the highway bridge on the RDB. You can tie up here at the William Stratton State Park Boat Launch for a while and visit the town of Morris. The sign at this dock stipulates a 15-minute tie-up limit. Near the bridge, there is also a small bait and tackle shop that sells snacks.

Morris is much smaller than Joliet. Nonetheless, you can find many of your needs here: a restaurant, post office, banks, laundromat, and auto-parts store. The grocery, D&S Foods, is open 24 hours. It is only one block north of the river, on the same street supported by the bridge.

Daniel Cook, a visionary Illinois legislator, first proposed a canal connecting the Great Lakes to the Gulf of Mexico in 1822. After several failed legislative attempts, Cook's Illinois and Michigan Canal (I & M Canal) was finally approved as a national project in 1827, just before Cook departed Congress. Furthermore, Daniel Cook was more than instrumental in establishing Illinois as an anti-slavery state. In many regards, he was the torch bearer for Abraham Lincoln, one generation later.

Between 1836 and 1848, the I & M Canal was dug by hand with mostly Irish immigrant laborers. These immigrants worked 15-hour days for a one dollar per day plus a ration of whiskey. This canal ran from La Salle, Illinois to a small lakeside settlement called Chicago. In 1848, a 96-mile, 22-hour trip on the canal was extraordinarily fast. La Salle, Peru, Utica, Ottawa, Marseilles, Channahon, Lockport, and Morris sprang up as canal towns.

Unfortunately, the canal was short-lived, as newly constructed parallel railroads made it obsolete by the 1860s. But fortunately, the impact of the canal remained. The canal was a boon to Morris as an important agricultural center. A fair amount of grain still moves through Morris, much of it exported all over the world. You'll see Archer-Daniels-Midland's presence in those many elevators along this river. The canal is especially well-preserved in Morris, and it sits about 15 feet higher than the current Illinois River.

There is a camping area with three boat ramps (no docks) about one and a half miles downriver from Morris on the RDB. The town of Seneca is about 10 miles downriver from Morris and also on the RDB or north side. Several locals have stated that a six-foot difference in the Illinois River water level is common through one season around Seneca.

Unlike Morris, the commercial district of Seneca is nearly a mile away from the river. Nevertheless, there are a handful of boating facilities along the Illinois River near Seneca. These facilities include Custom Marine, Boondocks Restaurant, Black's Marine, Hidden Cove Marina, and Spring Brook Marina on the LDB. Seneca Boat Club and Mariner's Village and Marina are on the RDB. Our drawing depicts this two-mile marina section near Seneca.

Custom Marine is developing its two basins, near mile marker 253 on the LDB, for

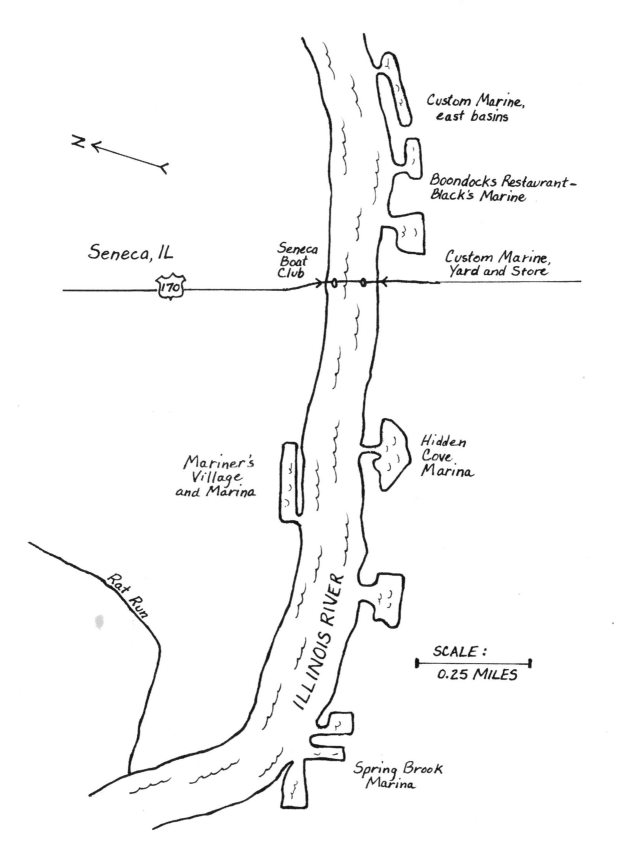

expanded recreational boating uses. Some of this development will be geared to transient boats in the 35-40-foot range. We were told that in 2001 eight slips near 40 feet long were built.

Boondocks Restaurant and Black's Marine are part of the same operation. Both are accessible from the towboat that is side-tied in the river at mile 252.8. The towboat is plumbed to distribute gasoline to recreational boaters. The third basin, immediately upriver from the highway bridge, near mile 252.7, houses Boondocks Restaurant, Black's Marine, and Custom Marine's well-stocked ship's store, maintenance area, and about a dozen slips. Custom Marine also has a yard and a 60-ton open-ended travel lift in this area.

The Seneca Boat Club is across the river from Custom Marine. The boat club has a clubhouse, boat ramp, and four small private docks. The Seneca Boat Club has the best location to access the town of Seneca, which has a few restaurants, a library, hardware store, pharmacy, and grocery store. These facilities are all on the main road and within a mile from the bridge. Without a computer aboard, I had a frequent compulsion to access the Internet, and I found that all public libraries in Illinois afforded me this opportunity.

Black's Marina/Boondocks Restaurant
   (815) 357-6666

Accepts transients—not encouraged
Floating towboat—yes
Ice—yes
Gasoline—yes (from the towboat)
Restaurant—on site

Custom Marine (815) 357-2628

Accepts transients—limited
Floating steel docks—yes

Dockside power connections—30 amp
Dockside water connections—yes
Showers—yes
Mechanical repairs—yes
Below-waterline repairs—yes
Ship's store—yes
Restaurant—nearby

Seneca Boat Club

Fixed steel docks—yes
Boat ramp—yes

Hidden Cove Marina is one-third of a mile downriver from the bridge on the LDB. Its surroundings are nice and shaded with trees, but the marina area is isolated from any other commercial attractions. Hidden Cove Marina has about 140 slips and is home to the Seneca Yacht Club. It offers Boat/US discounts.

Mariner's Village and Marina is in the basin on the RDB less than a quarter of a mile downriver from the entrance to Hidden Cove Marina. This is a modern facility on the Seneca side of the river. It is part of a private condominium complex with about 100 slips and a swimming pool. All of the slips at Mariner's Village and Marina are private.

Spring Brook Marina is a half-mile downriver from Mariner's Village back on the LDB. This very first class operation, with many amenities, is at mile 251.8. Spring Brook Marina has about 220 slips in three separate basin arms and can accommodate about an 80 footer. It also has a 50-ton travel lift and may have a courtesy car for transients.

Hidden Cove Marina (815) 357-6869

Approach depth—4-6 feet
Accepts transients—yes

Floating wooden piers—yes
Dockside power connections—30 and 50 amp
Dockside water connections—yes
Showers—yes
Gasoline—yes
Boat ramp—yes
Snack bar—seasonal

Mariner's Village and Marina (847) 956-7200

Accepts transients—no
Floating wooden piers—yes
Dockside power connections—30 amp
Dockside water connections—yes
Clubhouse—yes

Spring Brook Marina (815) 357-8666
http://www.springbrookmarina.com

Approach depth—7 feet
Accepts transients—yes
Floating steel docks—yes
Dockside power connections—30 and 50 amp
Dockside water connections—yes
Waste pump-out—yes
Showers—yes
Gasoline—yes
Mechanical repairs—yes
Below-waterline repairs—yes
Boat ramp—private
Ship's store—yes
Restaurant—on site

A cold morning on the docks at the South Shore Boat Club in Peru

CHAPTER 9

The Upper Illinois River, from Marseilles to Chillicothe

Our drawing depicts the 70-mile section of Illinois River covered in this chapter. The Marseilles Lock and Dam is about four and half miles downriver from Spring Brook Marina. There is a quaint little boat ramp with two small docks in a cove on the LDB about a half-mile upriver from the dam. Snug Harbor Marina, with about 14 slips, is also a half-mile upriver from the dam but on the RDB at mile 247.4.

Snug Harbor Marina (815) 795-9080

Dockside depth—7 feet
Accepts transients—yes, if patronizing
    lounge/restaurant
Floating wooden piers—yes
Gasoline—yes
Boat ramp—private
Lounge/restaurant—on site (dinner on weekends,
    lunch more often)

The Marseilles Dam blocks the Illinois River at mile 247.0 on the RDB, but the lock is two and a half miles downstream at mile 244.6. A narrow channel on the LDB leads to this lock. Bell's Island separates this channel from the main body of the Illinois River. The lock tenders monitor VHF 14 and their phone number is (815) 795-2593. The drop or lift at this lock is usually around 25 feet. The following table lists the bridges and locks covered in this chapter.

The entrance to Four Star Marina is slightly more than two and half miles downriver from the Marseilles Lock on the RDB. This entry is not well marked, nor can you spot the marina from the Illinois River. The marina is farther back in the small creek than where it's depicted on the Corps of Engineers chart. Four Star Marina has a campground and about 150 slips and offers Boat/US discounts.

Four Star Marina (815) 434-1748

Approach depth—7 feet
Accepts transients—yes
Floating steel docks—yes
Dockside power connections—15 and 30 amp
Dockside water connections—yes
Waste pump-out—yes
Showers—yes
Laundromat—yes
Gasoline—yes
Mechanical repairs—yes
Below-waterline repairs—yes
Boat ramp—yes
Ship's store—yes (small)
Restaurant—on site

The highway bridge at mile 239.7, two and a half miles downriver from Four Star Marina, marks the enchanting town of Ottawa, Illinois. The Fox River dumps into the Illinois River on the RDB just upriver from the bridge. The Fox River passes west of Chicago and originates near Milwaukee, Wisconsin. On August 21, 1858, the first of the seven Lincoln-Douglas debates was held in Ottawa's Washington Square. An estimated 40,000 people turned out to hear Mr. Lincoln's foreboding arguments against the evils of slavery. The founder of the Boy Scouts of America, William Boyce, is from Ottawa. The Ottawa Scouting Museum is one of the town's newest attractions.

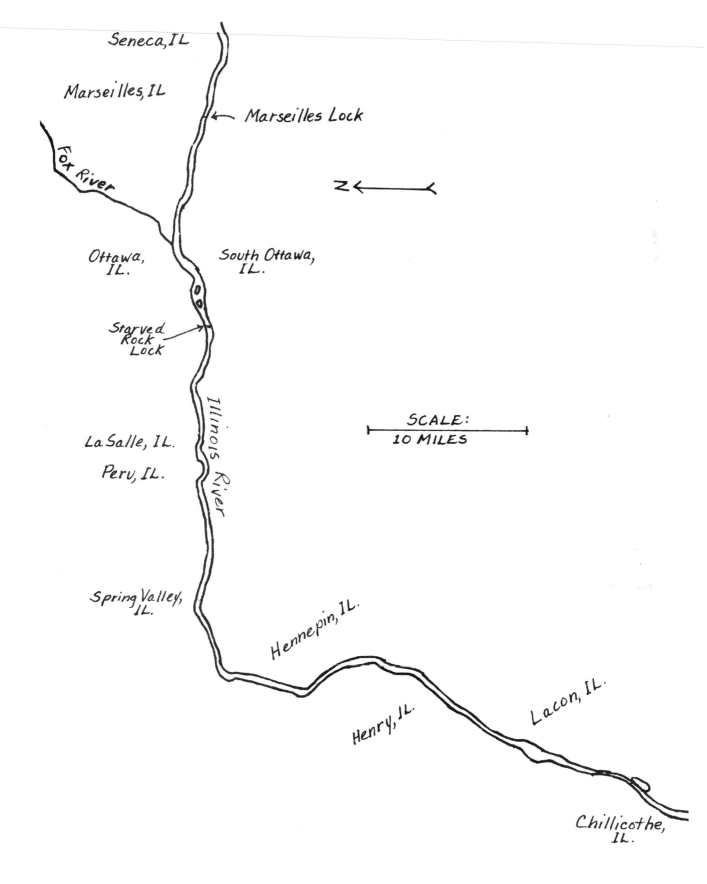

Seneca, IL

Marseilles, IL.

Marseilles Lock

Fox River

N

Ottawa, IL.

South Ottawa, IL.

Starved Rock Lock

Illinois River

SCALE:
10 MILES

La Salle, IL.

Peru, IL.

Spring Valley, IL.

Hennepin, IL.

Henry, IL.

Lacon, IL.

Chillicothe, IL.

BRIDGE NAME	TYPE	VERTICAL CLEARANCE (FEET)*		APPROX RIVER MILE
		CLOSED	UNIMPEDED	
Route 170, Seneca	Fixed	47	47	252.7
Marseilles Highway	Fixed	46	**46**	**246.9**
Marseilles Lock	Lock			244.6
Route 23, Ottawa	Fixed	47	47	239.7
Burlington Northern Railroad	Lift	**21**	47	**239.4**
Starved Rock Lock and Dam	Lock			231.0
Route 178, Utica	Fixed	62	62	229.6
Interstate 39	Fixed	66	66	225.8
Illinois Central Railroad	Fixed	61	61	225.6
Route 351, La Salle	Lift	26	81	224.8
Route 251, Peru	Fixed	62	62	222.9
Route 89, Spring Valley	Fixed	60	60	218.4
Interstate 180, Hennepin	Fixed	59	59	207.9
Route 26, Hennepin	Fixed	59	59	207.6
Route 18, Henry	Fixed	59	59	196.0
Route 17, Lacon	Fixed	59	59	189.1
Atchison, Topeka & Santa Fe Railroad	Fixed	58	58	181.9

*Clearance is for normal pool. High water, according to the *U.S. Coast Pilot,* could be 9-22 feet above normal pool.

There are four separate sets of nice public boat ramps around the highway bridge. I don't think there is any nicer selection of multiple boat ramps and docks anywhere else along the entire Illinois River than in Ottawa. The two ramps on the RDB have the best access to the town. The RDB dock almost beneath the bridge, and slightly in the Fox River, is very nice and has eight feet of water depth. This is a great docking location for a short-term tie-up and a visit to Ottawa. The town has many franchise restaurants, a grocery store, a hardware store, and a nice central city park. Ottawa is the largest Illinois River town since Joliet. Across the river on the LDB in South Ottawa, there are two sets of double ramps nestled in nice parks that have pavilions.

According to our cruising friends, Joe and Betsey Butera, there is a good anchorage on the RDB four and a half miles downriver from Ottawa. To arrive at this anchorage area, leave the Illinois River near mile 234.9 and head northeast into a large slough on the northwest side of Sheehan Island. The high cliffs at Buffalo Rock State Park will be to your northwest. Anchor anywhere in this area. There should be 12 to 15 feet of water depths in most areas. Joe and Betsey explored deep into this slough and found comfortable water depths well back.

Starved Rock Yacht Club is about a mile past Sheehan Island and also on the RDB. The private channel to the club is well marked by about 10 PVC posts painted with either green or red blazes. The hospitality was warm when we visited the Starved Rock Yacht Club. It has about 100 slips and 115 members. Larger Starved Rock Marina is about a half-mile downriver, also on the RDB. It has about 250 slips, a closed-ended 25-ton travel lift, and a boutique. Both the marina and the yacht club can accommodate 50 footers. At the marina, you can tie up at the docking area on the Illinois River to visit their restaurant or gasoline dock. Or you can also thread your way through the bending channel and obtain access to their large harbor. Like the Starved Rock Yacht Club, the marina has PVC-post navigation aids marking the sides of their channel. Even though the river is wide near these facilities, both are in their own well-protected harbors. Starved Rock State Park is across the river from the marina. You'll find another boat ramp in this park.

Starved Rock Yacht Club (815) 434-1553

Approach depth—5 feet
Dockside depth—5 feet
Accepts transients—yes
Floating steel docks—yes
Dockside power connections—30 amp
Dockside water connections—yes
Showers—yes
Laundromat—yes
Gasoline—yes
Boat ramp—yes
Restaurant—nearby

Starved Rock Marina (815) 433-4218
http://www.starvedrockmarina.com

Approach depth—5 feet
Dockside depth—5 feet
Accepts transients—yes
Floating wooden piers—yes
Dockside power connections—twin 30 amp
Dockside water connections—yes
Waste pump-out—yes
Showers—yes
Gasoline—yes
Diesel fuel—yes
Mechanical repairs—yes
Below-waterline repairs—yes
Boat ramp—yes
Ship's store—yes
Restaurant—on site

The shoreline topography along the Illinois River becomes steeper in this area. Bluffs, a few waterfalls, and canyons can be found. The legend of Starved Rock states that in 1760, a band of Illiniwek Indians were under attack by rival Ottawa Indians. The Illiniwek retreated and were planning to defend on a 125-foot sandstone bluff. But the Ottawa put the Illini under siege and starved them to death, thus the name Starved Rock. The Starved Rock Lock and Dam is slightly more than two miles downriver from the Starved Rock Marina. The dam is on the LDB, the lock on the RDB. The lock tenders monitor VHF 14 and can be reached at (815) 667-4114. The drop or lift at Starved Rock Lock is about 18 feet.

Starved Rock State Park extends for about seven miles on the LDB. In this park, there is a very nice boat ramp on the LDB immediately south of Plum Island, near mile 229.8. The seasonally open Starved Rock Canoe Rentals is next to, and downriver from, this boat ramp and upriver from the Utica

Highway Bridge. Past the Utica Bridge, in a four-mile stretch of river, there are four more bridges. Three are relatively high fixed but the third one is a lift bridge with about 26 feet of clearance in the closed position. The fourth bridge splits the neighboring RDB towns of La Salle and Peru.

The historic Illinois and Michigan Canal ends in La Salle, Illinois near mile 223.3 on the RDB. There is no RDB (or LDB) recreational-boat-friendly access to the town of La Salle, either in the entry to the Illinois and Michigan Canal or on the Illinois River. Any potential tie-up areas are industrially intimidating. Two ramps, but with no docks, can be found on the LDB south of the Peru Highway Bridge near mile 222.8. The only place to tie up to visit either La Salle or Peru, Illinois is at the South Shore Boat Club, on the north shore or the RDB, in Peru. This boat club was once located on the opposite, or south, shore. When the yacht club members moved to the present location, they retained their old name and relished the folly of the situation. The South Shore Boat Club has about 50 slips. The slips are small and exposed to the Illinois River, but if the club can fit you in somewhere on their docks, these folks proved to be very friendly and accommodating to transient boaters.

South Shore Boat Club (815) 223-9890

Approach depths—12 feet
Accepts transients—limited
Floating wooden piers—yes
Dockside power connections—limited 15 amp
Showers—yes
Gasoline—yes
Boat ramp—yes, but very steep
Restaurant—on site (seasonal)

The Spring Valley Boat Club is on the LDB three and a half miles downriver from Peru and the South Shore Boat Club. This hospitable private boat club is upriver from the Spring Valley Highway Bridge. The Spring Valley launch ramps are just downriver from the bridge. This launch area has three good ramps with short finger piers in a small semi-protected basin near mile 218.4 on the RDB. The town of Spring Valley, Illinois is about a half-mile north of these ramps.

Spring Valley Boat Club (815) 664-9096

Approach depth—6 feet
Accepts transients—yes
Floating wooden piers—yes (most covered)
Dockside power connections—30 amp
Dockside water connections—yes
Waste pump-out—yes
Showers—yes
Gasoline—yes
Boat ramp—yes
Clubhouse—yes (limited food)

After Spring Valley, the Illinois River continues to flow west. But eight miles west of Spring Valley, the river makes a 90-degree turn to the south. The Illinois River's confluence with the mighty Mississippi River is still 210 miles away, but now the Illinois flows mainly in a southerly direction. From here southward, with a few exceptions, a bridge usually signals a town on one side or the other of the river.

There are the remnants of an old canal near mile 210.3 on the RDB. The Hennepin Canal, built about a hundred years ago, once connected to the Rock River and then the Mississippi River. This barge canal was not in operation long because, once again, rail transportation rendered it obsolete. The Mississippi

River's Quad Cities of Davenport, Bettendorf (both in Iowa), Moline, and Rock Island (both in Illinois) are only about 70 miles from Hennepin via this old canal route. Some geologists believe that the Illinois River once flowed westward here to the Rock River. Later glacial action diverted the Illinois southward and to its present confluence with the Mississippi River.

The town of Hennepin is on the LDB and south of the two bridges. The town was named after Louis Hennepin. The downriver Hennepin Bridge is no longer in use. The nicest public docks on the entire Illinois River just might belong to the town of Hennepin. In Hennepin, we didn't notice any time-limit signs, as found on many other public docks. Nonetheless, transient boaters should not abuse the time they spend at this free public dock. This is a courtesy extended to us boaters from the obliging folks of Hennepin. If we abuse it, we'll likely lose this privilege of a one-night gratis tie-up.

Hennepin Visitor's Dock

Approach depth—7 feet
Floating aluminum docks—yes
Laundromat—nearby
Restaurant—several nearby

The town of Hennepin can be accessed southeast of the public docks by climbing the wooden steps up the bluff to the park gazebo. Hennepin is a small town; nonetheless, you might find everything you need within a

Grain silos across the river from Hennepin

The dock at Hennepin

Hennepin

stone's throw of the gazebo: a hardware store combined with a grocery store, a laundromat, a bait shop, and even a boat dealer, Hennepin Marine Sales. There are some restaurants in Hennepin, but they are a few blocks farther east. The public boat ramp in Hennepin is about a fifth of a mile south of the town dock area on the LDB. This area also has dual ramps and a few piers.

It's hard to beat the boating ambiance of Hennepin, but the town of Henry, Illinois is a very close contender. It is at the next bridge, about 11 miles downriver from Hennepin on the RDB at mile 196.0. Henry has a bona-fide marina and two public boat ramps with docks. The public dock on the upriver side of the bridge has a two-hour parking limit and can accommodate about a 20 footer. The Henry Harbor Landing Marina has about 80 slips, and the largest recreational vessels can side-tie outside of the marina basin on the 100-foot-long abandoned lockwall. The marina even provides utilities to this lockwall, but you do need long dock lines to reach the stakes near the lockwall. Many years ago, when Henry had that working lock and dam, the town was even more of a social gathering center. The old lockwall, the marina, and one of the public docking areas are on the upriver side of the bridge. The second public docking area, a lumber supply outlet, and the center of the town are on the downriver side of the bridge. Henry is about midway between Starved Rock and Peoria, and during the summer months, the town attracts many weekend boaters from both locales. The vibrant little town has two grocery stores, an auto-parts store, a hardware store, a few taverns, and an inviting city park.

Henry Harbor Landing Marina (309) 364-2181

Approach depth—10 feet
Accepts transients—yes
Floating steel and wooden docks—yes
Dockside power connections—30 amp
Dockside water connections—yes
Waste pump-out—yes
Showers—yes
Laundromat—nearby
Gasoline—yes
Diesel fuel—yes
Boat ramp—yes
Restaurant—on site

At mile 194.5 the channel becomes deceiving. The wider water heads to the southwest, but the narrower river channel heads to the left (south). There are many sloughs in this area, and most of the water is just out of sight. These sloughs and fertile waters attract many birds. If you're a bird watcher, you'll really begin to appreciate the Illinois River around here. From here southward you'll surely see scores of great blue herons, Canadian geese, cormorants, and great egrets. Luck permitting, you may even encounter bald eagles, wild turkeys, great horned owls, or turkey vultures. But don't lose track of the navigation aids; there are a few places where it would be easy to accidentally get your boat off track.

Lacon (rhymes with bacon) is seven miles downriver from Henry on the LDB and at the next bridge at mile 189.1. The best access to Lacon, Illinois is from inside the marina harbor and south of the bridge. In Lacon, you can find two small grocery stores, two drugstores, a few restaurants, an auto-parts store, a library, a few taverns, and a laundromat. The laundromat and Casey's gas station and general store are located within two blocks from the Morgan's Landing Marina.

Morgan's Landing Marina (309) 246-4149

Accepts transients—limited
Floating wooden piers—yes
Dockside power connections—15 and 30 amp
Dockside water connections—yes
Laundromat—nearby
Gasoline—yes
Boat ramp—yes
Restaurant—several nearby

Chillicothe, Illinois is eight and a half miles downriver from Lacon on the RDB near mile 180.5. There is no highway bridge over the river near Chillicothe, but there is a railroad bridge a couple of miles north of this town. There is a good dual concrete public boat ramp with a 200-foot floating wooden dock signaling Chillicothe. Bananas Beach Club sits south of this ramp. Chillicothe is a bit more spread out than most other river towns.

The main restaurant area is on the highway, several blocks away from the river. Nevertheless, central Chillicothe is only a few blocks from the river. This quaint central area has a library, a laundromat, two hardware stores, and a few eateries and taverns. The private Chillicothe Condominium Marina, with about 30 slips in a small basin, is near the south end of Chillicothe, near mile 179.9 on the RDB.

Chillicothe Condominium Marina

Approach depth—5 feet
Floating wooden piers—yes
Dockside power connections—30 amp
Dockside water connections—yes
Laundromat—nearby
Restaurant—several nearby

Crafts Fair on the Peoria waterfront

CHAPTER 10

The Peoria Area

The fertile Peoria Lakes area was known to Native Americans as Pimiteoui or "land of great abundance." In 1673, returning from a voyage down the Mississippi River, Marquette and Joliet entered this valley, and their reports of its bounteousness would change the area forever. In 1691, with the help of local Native Americans, the French built Fort Pimiteoui, and later the area was known as "Au Pe." This fort evolved into the first enduring European settlement in Illinois. The French and Indian War began in 1754. After the war, in 1763, the British gained control. Nevertheless, the French culture hung on and Peoria thrived. Like nearly everywhere in the "West," French colonists supported the upstart Americans in their fight against the British during the Revolutionary War. In 1783, immediately after the Revolution, the Americans treated the French and local Indians well. But that didn't last long. By 1812, the growing American population wiped out the Native Americans and then rousted and deported the French to an uninhabited wilderness area near Alton, Illinois. Illinois became a state in 1818, and an even greater tide of "American immigrants" entered the Illinois Valley.

American industries such as meat packing, foundries, and distilleries evolved. Peoria also became a rail hub. By 1900, the abundance of corn and clear water helped make Peoria the "Whiskey Capital of the World." Today, Peoria is the second largest metropolitan area in Illinois and home to many industries. One of the more respected and internationally known companies based in Peoria is the Caterpillar Corporation.

The Illinois River widens to lakelike proportions—close to two miles wide at places—about 17 miles north of Peoria. Upper Peoria Lake is about 12 miles long. At the south end of Upper Peoria Lake, the Illinois River chokes for about a mile before it enters Peoria Lake. Smaller Peoria Lake is about three miles long and one mile wide. The Illinois River flows out of Peoria Lake at the southwest corner near downtown Peoria. Our drawing depicts the waters of this greater Peoria area. In addition to providing you with some of the typical river mile markers to describe the locations of boating facilities on these lakes, we'll provide you with GPS way points because we feel that these are more practical for the two lakes around Peoria. If you insist on all Peoria Lake river miles, you can find them in Appendix B. In any event, it behooves you to stay in the Illinois River Channel through these lakes, especially during times of low water.

The Illinois River Channel continues to be well marked in this two-lake area. Besides the normal floating buoyage system, there are nearly a score of 20-30-feet concrete navigational towers on the lakes. These towers are very useful additional navigational aids, but striking a tower with a boat (i.e., in reduced-visibility conditions) would have a disastrous consequence on the boat. Furthermore, some of these towers have partially submerged rocks extending some distance from the base. We also observed, at a time of relatively low water level in the fall, that the depth of the lakes,

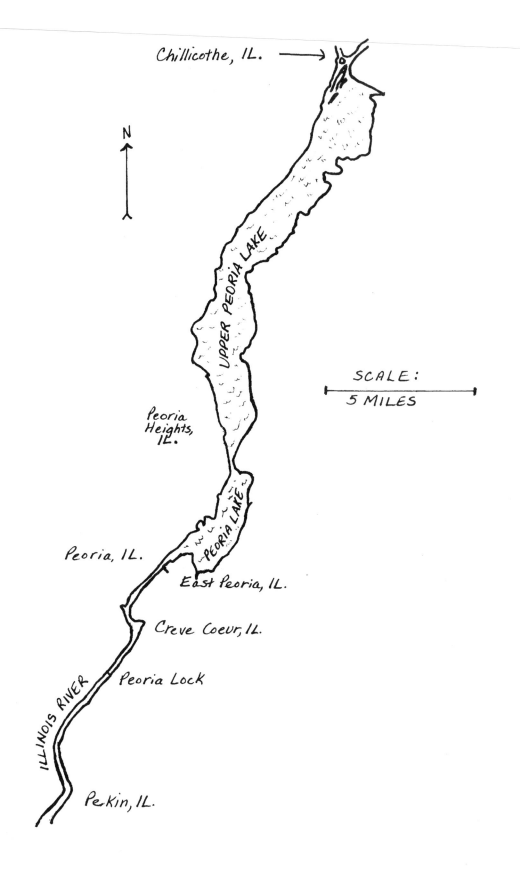

Chillicothe, IL.

N

UPPER PEORIA LAKE

SCALE:
5 MILES

Peoria
Heights,
IL.

PEORIA LAKE

Peoria, IL.

East Peoria, IL.

Creve Coeur, IL.

ILLINOIS RIVER

Peoria Lock

Pekin, IL.

outside of the Illinois River Channel, seldom exceeded five feet. Nonetheless, these five-foot soundings seemed to be consistent throughout most of the lakes except close to the shore, where the water depth naturally shallowed. In the spring, after the snow melts upstream, the water levels in these lakes, as well as on all of the Illinois River, can rise dramatically.

Our next drawing shows Upper Peoria Lake and the locations of various marinas. Soon after entering Upper Peoria Lake, and after passing the first 30-foot-tall navigation aid, you come to the entrance of Hamm's Holiday Harbor Marina, on the RDB near river mile 178.6. The north side of the entry is slightly bottlenecked with some worn-out and hard-aground barges. The entry isn't all that wide. There is a shallow shoal on the south side of the Hamm's Harbor entry and this shoal may be marked with unofficial navigation aids. In any event, don't stray too far from those barges or the north side of the channel in order to stay in the deeper water. Hamm's has about 150 slips and can accommodate fairly big transient boats. The facility has two travel lifts—a 35-ton and a 50-ton—and they also work on commercial barges.

Hamm's Holiday Harbor Marina (309) 696-2178

Approach depth—5 feet
Accepts transients—yes
Floating concrete docks—yes
Dockside power connections—15, 30, and 50 amp
Dockside water connections—yes
Showers—yes
Gasoline—yes
Below-waterline repairs—yes
Boat ramp—yes
Restaurant—on site

About nine miles down the Illinois River Channel, and after about 10 more tall day-marks, you'll be approaching Peoria Heights on the RDB. Near Illinois River mile 169.5, you'll find two marinas on the RDB—National Marine North Marina and the Whitecap Drifters Boat Club. To arrive at National Marine North, leave the channel near GPS way point 40.46.22N/89.33.69W and head for the old Phillips 66 gas sign. As you get close, this sign will be on the north side of the entry. National Marine North is primarily an out-of-water boat storage facility, with a 30-ton open-ended travel lift. For the Whitecap Drifters Boat Club, leave the channel near GPS way point 40.46.15N/89.33.62W and head for the RDB and the marina entry. This is a very small facility with about 10 slips and limited to accommodating nothing much bigger than 20 feet. The boat club also has a campground. We found about five feet of water after we departed the main channel to the breakwaters of both marina entrances.

National Marine North Marina (309) 688-5513

Approach depth—5 feet
Accepts transients—very limited
Floating steel and wooden docks—yes
Dockside power connections—15 and 30 amp
Dockside water connections—yes
Showers—yes
Below-waterline repairs—yes

Whitecap Drifters Boat Club (309) 691-5600

Approach depth—5 feet
Floating plastic docks—yes
Boat ramp—yes
Clubhouse—seasonal

There are three more boating facilities in Peoria Heights about a mile and a half downriver on the RDB. The northernmost one is National Marine South Marina. To arrive

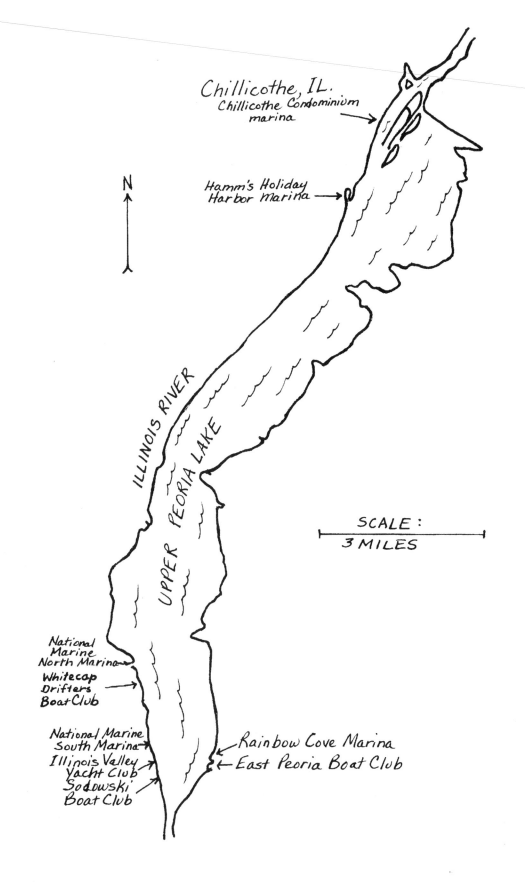

Chillicothe, IL.
Chillicothe Condominium marina

N

Hamm's Holiday Harbor Marina

ILLINOIS RIVER

UPPER PEORIA LAKE

SCALE :
3 MILES

National Marine North Marina
Whitecap Drifters Boat Club

National Marine South Marina
Illinois Valley Yacht Club
Sodowski Boat Club

Rainbow Cove Marina
East Peoria Boat Club

here, leave the RDB side of the Illinois River Channel near GPS way point 40.45.21N/89.33.38W. The marina has one of the bigger boatyards and haul-out accommodations in this area.

The second facility is the Illinois Valley Yacht Club, commonly known as "IVY." It likely has more amenities, including a swimming pool, than any other boat club on the Illinois River. There are two entrances (north and south). The fuel dock, restaurant, and clubhouse are approached from the north entry, or north harbor. Leave the main Illinois River Channel near this GPS way point 40.44.90N/89.33.17W, and then take a heading of 245 degrees to this northern entrance. There are more than 400 feet of barges between the entrances. These two barges, connected bow to stern, are an excellent place for some of the largest transiting vessels (too lengthy to enter the harbor) to tie up. There are also plenty of dockside utilities on the barges. Some of the smaller transient vessels may be directed to the south entry of the Illinois Valley Yacht Club, where there are plenty of smaller slips. The IVY Club is the first facility south of Lake Michigan that organizes regular sailboat races.

The Sodowski Boat Club is about 150 yards south of the IVY. Leave the main channel at GPS way point 40.44.80N/89.33.22W, and then head for the entry into Sodowski's protected breakwater. This entry is at the southeast corner of the facility. Both Sodowski's and National Marine South have about 40-50 slips. IVY, by far the most comprehensive facility in the area, has nearly 190 slips and can accommodate a 60 footer in certain slips and at least a 100 footer tied up to the barges.

National Marine South Marina (309) 688-5513
http://www.nationalboats.com

Approach depth—5 feet
Accepts transients—limited
Floating vinyl decking—yes
Dockside power connections—30 amp
Dockside water connections—yes
Waste pump-out—yes
Gasoline—yes
Mechanical repairs—limited
Below-waterline repairs—limited
Boat ramp—yes
Ship's store—yes

Illinois Valley Yacht Club (IVY) (309) 682-5419

Approach depth—5 feet
Accepts transients—yes
Floating vinyl decking—yes
Dockside power connections—twin 30 amp and 50 amp
Dockside water connections—yes
Waste pump-out—yes
Showers—yes
Laundromat—yes
Gasoline—yes
Diesel fuel—yes
Boat ramp—yes
Restaurant—on site

Sodowski Boat Club (309) 688-2526

Approach depth—5 feet
Accepts transients—limited
Floating wooden piers—yes
Dockside power connections—30 amp
Dockside water connections—yes
Showers—yes
Laundromat—yes
Gasoline—yes
Mechanical repairs—yes
Below-waterline repairs—10-ton hoist on a railway only
Ship's store—yes (limited)

The Rainbow Cove Marina and the East Peoria Boat Club are on the opposite, east, side of Upper Peoria Lake. Both facilities are about a mile and a half across Upper Peoria Lake from the Illinois Valley Yacht Club. The northernmost facility is Rainbow Cove Marina. Arrive at way point 40.44.91N/89.32.26W, well off the main channel, then head into the Rainbow channel, which is marked by three PVC pipes. Rainbow Cove Marina has about 100 slips. The East Peoria Boat Club, in a brand-new facility, is about half that size. Both facilities can accommodate 40 footers. The entrance to the East Peoria Boat Club is about 250 yards south-southwest of the entrance to Rainbow Cove Marina. The boat club also has a well-marked entrance after you arrive at this way point—40.44.78N/89.32.38W. A spit of land is to the north of this channel, and two white buoys mark the five-foot deep channel. The hospitality we encountered at the East Peoria Boat Club was outstanding. We were invited to an evening cookout where savory "rock soup" was being served out of a steaming caldron.

Rainbow Cove Marina (309) 698-0216

Approach depth—5 feet
Dockside depth—5 feet
Accepts transients—yes
Floating steel and wooden docks—yes
Dockside power connections—30 amp
Dockside water connections—yes
Showers—yes
Mechanical repairs—yes
Below-waterline repairs—yes
Boat ramp—private
Ship's store—yes

East Peoria Boat Club (309) 699-6655

Approach depth—5 feet
Dockside depth—5 feet
Accepts transients—yes
Floating steel and wooden docks—yes
Dockside power connections—20 and 30 amp
Dockside water connections—yes
Showers—yes

Gasoline—yes
Boat ramp—yes
Clubhouse—yes

Upper Peoria Lake constricts about one and a half miles south of the Sodowski and East Peoria boat clubs. A relatively narrow chute, about a mile in length, connects Upper Peoria Lake to Peoria Lake. The north end of Peoria Lake is at river mile 166.1. The bright blue McClugage Highway bridge is near the north end of the lake and about a quarter-mile south of the narrows. The following table lists the bridges and locks covered in this chapter.

There are five boating facilities and a casino boat on Peoria Lake. The three facilities on the RDB are Wharf Harbor Marina, Detweiller's Municipal Marina, and the Peoria Boat Club. The Peoria Boat Club is tucked in the western end of the large harbor housing Detweiller's Municipal Marina. Detweiller's Marina and Wharf Harbor are about a mile and a half apart. The entrance to Wharf Harbor Marina is well buoyed with four red floats. Leave the RDB side of the channel near this way point—40.42.67N/89.33.08W. After you enter the harbor, the fuel dock, ramp, and travel-lift bay are to your south. The marina also has a well-stocked ship's store and the grounds are well maintained. The highly recommended Alexander Street Steak House is next to the marina.

The entrance to Detweiller's Municipal Marina and Peoria Boat Club is near river mile 163.7. Depart the RDB side of the channel at way point 40.41.91N/89.34.06W and in about six feet of water depth. Detweiller's is in a slightly larger protected cove than Wharf Harbor Marina. The Detweiller harbor is also the closest marina area to downtown Peoria. Detweiller's

BRIDGE NAME	TYPE	VERTICAL CLEARANCE (FEET)*		APPROX RIVER MILE
		CLOSED	UNIMPEDED	
A., T. &Santa Fe Railroad, Chillicothe	Fixed	58	58	181.9
U.S. Routes 24 &150, Peoria Lake	Fixed	65	65	165.8
Interstate 74, Peoria	Fixed	65	65	162.8
Bob Michel Highway, Peoria	Fixed	63**	63	162.2
Cedar Street Bridge, Peoria	Fixed	78	78	161.6
Pekin Union Railroad, Peoria	Lift	**19**	66	**160.7**
Interstate 474	Fixed	64	64	157.9
Peoria Lock and Dam	Lock			157.7
Route 9, Pekin	Fixed	72	72	152.9

*Clearance is for normal pool. High water, according to the *U.S. Coast Pilot,* could be 7-17 feet above normal pool.

**U.S. Coast Pilot* indicates only a 31-foot clearance bascule bridge

Marina has about 200 slips; Wharf Harbor has about 150 slips; and the smaller Peoria Boat Club has 36 slips. Wharf Harbor also has two travel lifts—a 15-ton closed- and a 30-ton open-ended lift. Our drawing depicts the locations of the marinas on Peoria Lake and shows a portion of downtown Peoria on the Illinois River.

Wharf Harbor Marina (309) 688-4141

Approach depth—5 feet
Accepts transients—yes
Floating steel and wooden docks—yes (covered)
Dockside power connections—twin 30 amp
Dockside water connections—yes
Waste pump-out—yes
Showers—yes
Gasoline—yes
Mechanical repairs—yes
Below-waterline repairs—yes
Boat ramp—yes

Ship's store—yes
Restaurant—on site

Detweiller's Municipal Marina (309) 657-0697

Approach depth—5 feet
Accepts transients—yes
Floating wooden piers—yes
Dockside power connections—15 and 30 amp
Dockside water connections—yes
Showers—yes
Gasoline—yes
Boat ramp—yes

Peoria Boat Club (309) 676-9485

Approach depth—5 feet
Accepts transients—yes
Floating concrete docks—yes
Dockside power connections—30 amp
Dockside water connections—yes

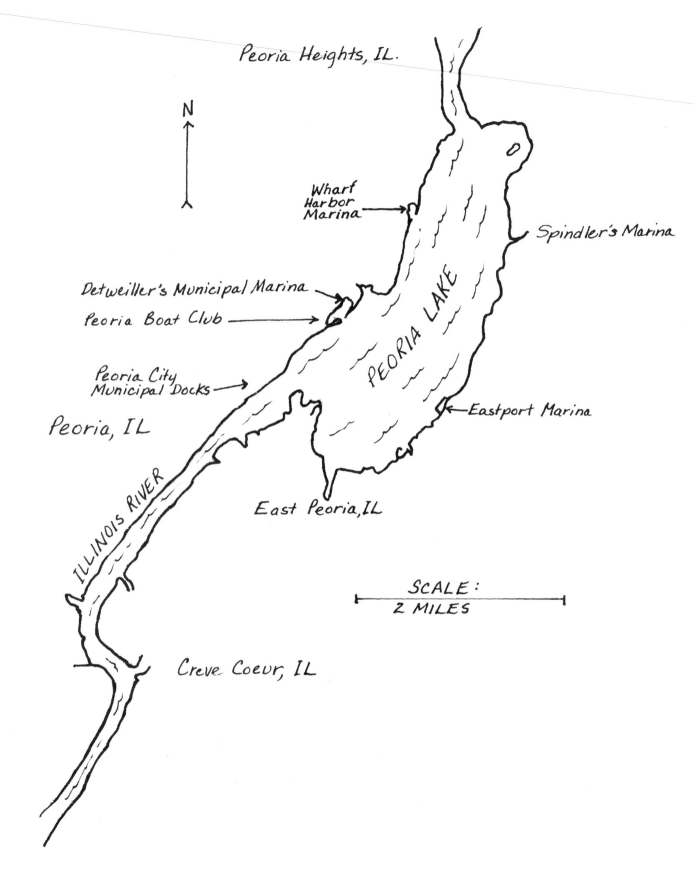

Showers—yes
Boat ramp—yes
Clubhouse—yes

The two marinas on the LDB of Peoria Lake are Spindler's Marina and Campground and the Eastport Marina. They are also about a mile and a half apart. Spindler's is right across Peoria Lake from Wharf Harbor Marina. Eastport is nearly right across the lake from Detweiller's. To enter Spindler's, position yourself on the LDB side of the channel at way point 40.42.65N/89.32.67W. Spindler's well-marked channel has six floating orange and white buoys leading to a small protected basin. Spindler's is more a campground than a marina, with about 40 slips and only capable of handling boats under 25 feet. Spindler's does store many trailerable boats on site.

Spindler's Marina and Campground
(309) 699-3549

Approach depth—5 feet
Accepts transients—yes
Floating concrete docks—yes
Showers—yes
Boat ramp—yes (triple)
Variety store—limited
Snack bar—limited

Eastport Marina is not in a natural harbor, but instead protected by a large manmade floating breakwater extending into the lake. Eastport Marina is part of a larger first-class facility that holds a restaurant, pool, and condominium complex. The marina portion has about 250 slips and can accommodate 90 footers. Depart the LDB side of the channel at way point 40.41.84N/89.33.30W and enter the well-buoyed channel marked with six "official-looking" navigation aids leading to

the entrance of the manmade Eastport Marina harbor. After you enter the opening in the floating breakwater, the fuel dock and Famous Dave's Barbecue Restaurant are situated at the southwest corner and inside the protected waters. The showy Par-a-Dice Casino Boat is located less than a mile southwest of the Eastport Marina Harbor, also on the LDB.

Eastport Marina (309) 694-3034

Approach depth—5 feet
Accepts transients—yes
Floating wooden piers—yes
Dockside power connections—30 and 50 amp
Dockside water connections—yes
Waste pump-out—yes
Showers—yes
Laundromat—yes
Gasoline—yes
Diesel fuel—yes
Mechanical repairs—yes
Below-waterline repairs—yes
Boat ramp—private
Ship's store—nearby
Restaurant—on site and four nearby

Peoria Lake chokes down in the western end and gives way to downtown Peoria, the heart of which is located on the RDB between the next two bridges. Peoria, Illinois has some charming municipal docks and a visitor center for visiting boaters. Although these docks have electricity, they are not intended for overnight tying up. The hourly slippage is expensive: for vessels over 28 feet, it costs $2 per hour; for vessels 28 feet and less, it's $1 per hour. There are a total of about 60 slips in two separate sections. The 121-foot-long paddlewheeler, *Spirit of Peoria*, divides these two sections. The first steamboat to arrive in Peoria was the *Liberty* in 1829. By 1850, more than 1,200 vessels had been calling on the Port of

Peoria. Downtown Peoria is a most stimulating stopping point.

Peoria City Municipal Docks (309) 494-8851

Accepts transients—yes, but not overnight
Floating concrete docks—yes
Dockside power connections—15 and 30 amp
Dockside water connections—yes
Restaurant—3 nearby

We've been told that many boats anchor out for the night near the opposite bank (the LDB). A Wal-Mart is located behind that brush line on the LDB. This is likely your closest Wal-Mart on any river between Chicago and Mobile. To get to it, you'd need to land your dinghy on that rocky LDB and then work your way through the 40 yards of brush. Depending how your boating/household supplies are holding out, it may be worth it. A U.S. Coast Guard station sits in the LDB cove west of the Wal-Mart and east of the Steak and Shake Restaurant. The sprawling Caterpillar Tractor plant is situated on acres of land on the LDB in East Peoria south of the second highway bridge, the Bob Michel Bridge. The main Peoria post office is across the river on the RDB. Downtown Peoria starts fading around river mile 162.0.

The Illinois River in Peoria

Floodwall and Riverwalk in Peoria

Peoria City Municipal Docks, with *Spirit of Peoria* in the distance

You'll find the Creve Coeur concrete launching ramp and a small dock at mile 159.2 on the LDB. Nearby, Fort Crevecoeur (French for broken heart) was established by explorer Robert Cavalier de La Salle in 1680. The fort was the very first European building in "Middle America," but it was mysteriously abandoned after only four months. There are other ghosts of French forts on this trip south. Fort St. Louis was built near Starved Rock. The city of St. Louis itself once was a French fort; and Fort Massac is on the Ohio River. During the first century of European settlement, the French colonists dominated this area.

Fitzpatrick's Landing Restaurant is just south of the Creve Coeur ramp, and the restaurant has about 60 feet of dock frontage. A fixed interstate highway bridge, I-474, crosses the Illinois River at mile 157.9. The Peoria Lock and Dam is less than a quarter-mile downriver. The dam is on the RDB, and the lock is on the LDB. The lock tenders monitor VHF 14 and can be telephoned at (309) 699-6111. The drop or lift at Peoria Lock is only about eight feet, but the river barge traffic is likely to become heavier downriver from Peoria. After we depart the Peoria Lock, we'll find another wide concrete boat ramp two miles downriver at 155.5 on the RDB.

Kampsville ferry, heading across the Illinois River

CHAPTER 11

The Lower Illinois River, from Pekin to Grafton

South of Peoria, the Illinois River becomes much less developed. The shoreline is often sandy or treelined. Sometimes levees will follow the shoreline for many miles. There may be an occasional power plant along the river, but nothing like the development along the Upper Illinois. Our drawings depict the Illinois River coverage in this chapter. The first covers the river from Pekin to Meredosia, or the northern part. The second depicts the river between Meredosia to Grafton, or the southern section.

Pekin, Illinois, on the LDB, is 10 miles downriver from Peoria and about five miles downriver from Peoria Lock. Sen. Everett Dirkson is Pekin's favorite son. He was anything but taciturn; in the Senate he was often referred to as the "Silver Tongued Orator." There are a few marginal places to tie up around Pekin. The Pekin Boat Club and Trailer Park has a dicey 50-foot dock facing the Illinois River on the western side of Cooper's Island. The canal on the northwest side of the island is the location for transient boaters. Contrary to what is shown on the charts, this canal does not connect to the other side of the Illinois Channel. We found about six feet of water about halfway in this canal cut and there is a boat ramp at the head of the canal. The southeast entrance to the canal around Cooper's Island is very shallow and treacherous with many rocks.

Pekin Boat Club and Trailer Park (309) 346-9133

Approach depth—6 feet
Accepts transients—yes
Floating steel docks—yes (at fuel dock)
Dockside power connections—seasonal
Dockside water connections—seasonal
Showers—yes
Gasoline—seasonal
Mechanical repairs—yes (independent contractor)
Boat ramp—yes
Clubhouse—seasonal

There is also a concrete launch ramp across the Illinois River from Cooper's Island with no dock. We found another launch ramp with a short dock just south of the highway bridge on the LDB. This ramp and dock have the best access to Pekin, but the access is marginal. In Pekin, there are a few restaurants within a couple of blocks of the river.

The following table lists the bridges, locks, ferries, and major river confluences covered in this chapter.

Near Kingston Mines, and seven and a half miles south of Pekin at river mile 145.5 on the RDB, there is a ramp but with no dock. There is another concrete narrow ramp with no dock on the RDB at mile 136.7, a half-mile south of Copperas Creek. At mile 128.1 on the RDB, you can find a double concrete ramp with two wooden docks nearly 25 feet long. The small residential village of Liverpool, Illinois sits beyond the docks and the levee. Helle's Riverview Inn is about the only attraction in Liverpool. The inn, open seasonally, is situated on the south side of the road just beyond the levee. The levee will extend for many miles on the RDB. Quiver Beach has a fairly nice beach and bungalow

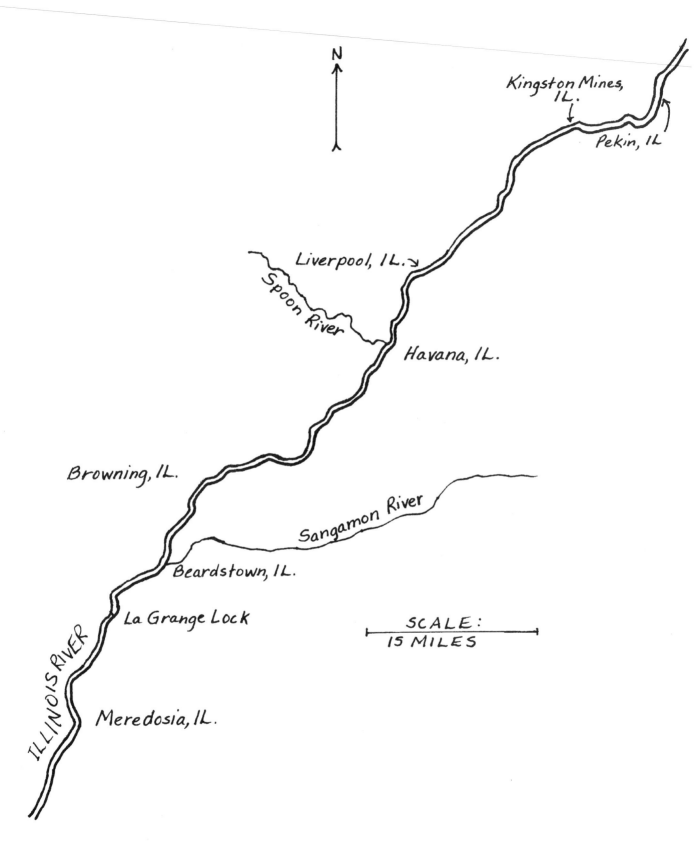

N

Kingston Mines, IL.

Pekin, IL

Liverpool, IL.

Spoon River

Havana, IL.

Browning, IL.

Sangamon River

Beardstown, IL.

La Grange Lock

ILLINOIS RIVER

Meredosia, IL.

SCALE:
15 MILES

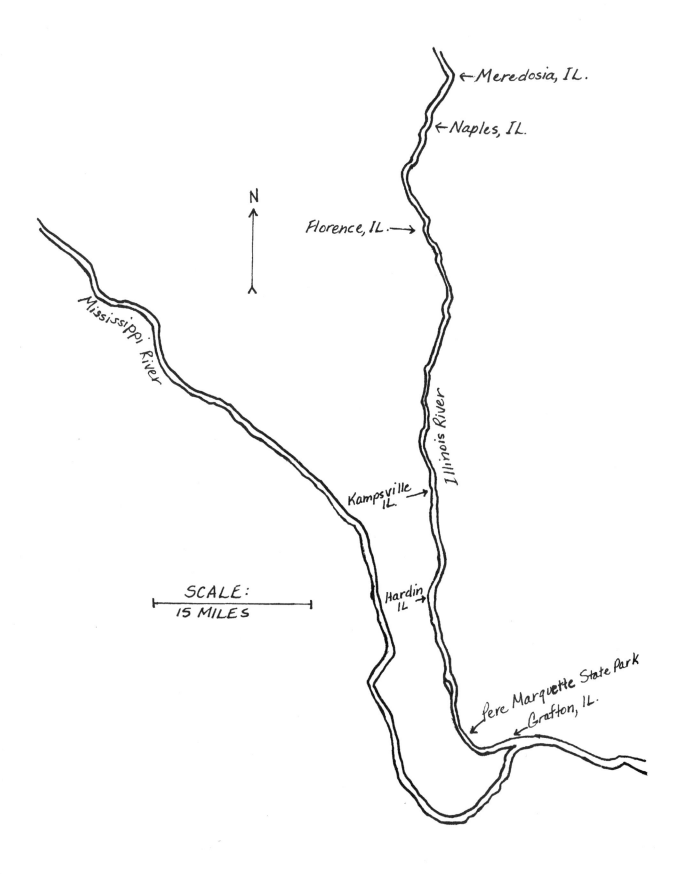

BRIDGE NAME	TYPE	VERTICAL CLEARANCE (FEET)*		APPROX RIVER MILE
		CLOSED	UNIMPEDED	
Route 9, Pekin	Fixed	72	72	152.9
Union Pacific Railroad	Lift	30**	71	151.2
U.S. Route 136, Havana	Fixed	67**	70	119.5
Burlington North Santa Fe Railroad	Lift	**19***	68	**88.8**
U.S. Routes 67 & 100, Beardstown	Fixed	68	68	87.9
La Grange Lock and Dam	Lock			80.2
Routes 99 & 104, Meredosia	Fixed	72	72	71.3
Norfolk and Southern Railroad	Lift	32	77	61.3
U.S. Route 36, Valley City	Fixed	71	71	60.2
Routes 100 & 106, Florence	Lift	26	82	56.0
Gateway Western Railroad	Lift	20	69	43.2
Kampsville Ferry, Kampsville	Ferry			32.1
Routes 16 & 100, Hardin	Lift	25	65	21.5
Confluence with Mississippi River				0.0

*Clearance is for normal pool. High water, according to the *U.S. Coast Pilot,* could be 16-26 feet above normal pool.

**Corps of Engineers charts indicate three to four extra feet of clearance

*****U.S. Coast Pilot* indicates a 54-foot clearance lift bridge

area near mile 122.5 on the LDB. The Spoon River enters the Illinois River at mile 120.5 on the RDB a half-mile upstream from Havana. The highway bridge at Havana is at mile 119.5. Most of historic Havana, Illinois sits north of the bridge on the LDB (i.e., between mile 119.5 and 120.2). The nicest ramp in town, and with a boat dock, is at mile 120.2. This is the best place for access to Havana's IGA grocery store, ACE hardware store, and a few restaurants and taverns. Havana, like its namesake in Cuba, was a rip-roaring place until the 1950s. The attraction was riverboat gambling. Havana still has many nice cobblestone streets and the oldest working water tower in Illinois.

Back on the Illinois River, the Belle of the Night Riverboat Restaurant is south (downriver) from this ramp. There is another nice double boat ramp with a dock, and four feet of water, on the south side of the bridge at mile 119.4 on the LDB. It's about a half-mile walk to Havana from this dock. There is a floodwall north of this ramp and dock, which is sometimes used as an embarking and alighting area for crew members aboard some of the river towboats.

There is an unimproved steep concrete boat ramp, with no dock, at mile 108.3 on the

RDB. A white grain silo right on the river sits near this Holmes Landing Boat Ramp. Fellow cruisers Dawn and Sam Vaura found an anchorage at mile 106.3 on the LDB. Dawn and Sam entered this slough and found about seven feet of water less than 50 yards into the creek.

There is another concrete boat ramp, with no dock, at mile 98.7 on the RDB. At mile 97.4 on the RDB, you'll find another twin concrete ramp and a small floating fuel barge. This is part of the seasonally opened River's Edge Boat Club near Browning, Illinois. There is only enough room for about one 30 footer to tie off at this fuel barge.

River's Edge Boat Club (217) 323-4780

Approach depth—6 feet
Accepts transients—space-available basis
Floating steel fuel barge—yes
Dockside power connections—30 amp
Gasoline—yes
Diesel fuel—yes
Boat ramp—yes
Restaurant—on site

At mile 91.6 on the RDB, beneath the power lines, there is a gravel boat ramp with no dock. This area looks a bit rough, with old pilings in the water.

The Sangamon River, originating near Springfield, Illinois, flows into the Illinois River at mile 88.9 on the LDB. In 1831, a young Abraham Lincoln and two compatriots boarded a crude flatboat loaded with pork in barrels, corn, and hogs for a long river trip. They started on the Sangamon River and were going all of the way to New Orleans. But the trip almost ended in a disaster on the Sangamon before Beardstown. Their boat got hung up on a mill dam and was nearly lost.

Abe's quick thinking and heads-up reactions saved the day . . . and the trip. Three weeks and 1,000 miles later, young Abe and his friends arrived in New Orleans. The cargo was safely delivered, and the onetime-trip boat was scrapped. Abe received about $70 for his effort before going on to even more noble achievements.

The town of Beardstown, Illinois is just beyond the Sangamon River entry on the LDB. South of the overhead power lines, you'll see a floating barge with a picnic table. Recreational boaters can tie up to this barge and visit Beardstown. We found the deeper water, about six feet deep, to be on the south side of this barge. We found no fuel on the river near this town. After tying off to the barge, climb the stairs over the floodwall and visit Beardstown. You will find an enchanting city square. Beardstown has a few fine restaurants, two grocery stores (one is Hispanic), a post office, library, and auto-parts store.

Beardstown City Dock Barge

Approach depth—6 feet (south side)
Floating steel barge—yes
Restaurant—several nearby

The highway bridge crosses the river immediately south of Beardstown. Fellow cruisers Betsey and Joe Butera found another anchorage at mile 85.5 on the LDB. The main river channel is on the RDB side here. Betsey and Joe found relatively deep water out of the main river channel close to the LDB shore less than a half-mile south of Bar Island.

The La Grange Lock and Dam is the southernmost one on the Illinois River. The dam is on the LDB and the lock on the RDB at mile 80.2. The La Grange Lock can be contacted on VHF

14 or at phone (217) 225-3317. The drop or lift at this lock is about 10 feet. Like all locks on the Illinois River, expect the lock master to throw two lines to your vessel. You will need to take up the slack, if lifting, or feed slack into the line, if you are dropping. Most of the turbulence in this particular lock is in the middle of the pit. Hence the lock master may request that you position your boat in the front portion of the lock.

The lowest two locks on the Illinois River, La Grange and Peoria locks, have a "high water sailing line" depicted on the Corps of Engineers charts. There are times, usually during the spring, when the water level is sufficiently high. For navigation, the locks are bypassed, and the Illinois River is "open water" over these dams. These "wicket dams" actually fold down onto the riverbed. If you're in doubt, always contact the lock tenders on the VHF or telephone beforehand.

In Meredosia, Illinois, the Naples Boat Club has no dock, although the club does have two ramps on the LDB about a fifth of a mile downriver from the highway bridge. Meredosia is situated on the LDB, in a bend in the river, at mile 71.2. It has a market, a laundromat, a couple of restaurants, a few gas stations, and a river museum. Stephen A. Douglas once practiced law in Meredosia. Later, he became the mouthpiece of the Democratic Party and was most capable of eloquently presenting the viewpoints of the pre-Civil War South.

Naples Boat Club (217) 584-1633

Laundromat—nearby
Boat ramp—yes
Restaurant—2 nearby

The small village of Naples is about five miles downriver from Meredosia on the LDB.

There is a private dock at Bruner Landing, mile 66.1 on the LDB. Another concrete ramp is a half-mile downriver from Bruner Landing and south of the power lines.

The Griggsville Landing Boat Ramp, at mile 61.2 on the RDB, has a 15-foot-long dock with about 10 feet of water depth. This area has a picnic grounds and is about five miles south of Naples. This is also the westernmost point of the entire "Great Circle." We are near longitude 90.39.00W. From this point to the Mississippi River, the Illinois River floodplain extends well past the LDB side. The RDB shore of the Illinois River is the western edge of this floodplain.

There is a very unimproved ramp at mile 57.3 on the RDB. Immediately after the highway bridge, there is another double concrete ramp with no dock at mile 55.8 on the RDB. We did not see any evidence of a town nearby, but the hamlet of Florence, Illinois supposedly is located somewhere west of this ramp. North of the Cargill elevator, at about mile 55.5 RDB, we encountered a 25-foot floating dock in about six feet of water in a campground area.

Between Florence and Kampsville (i.e., between river miles 54.0 and 38.0), there could be small underwater wing dams in the river. These submerged dams extend out from the shore and a fair ways into the river. In this section, it would be doubly prudent to keep your vessel near the center of the channel and especially avoid straying outside of the buoys. A line of rolling ripples on the water surface may indicate the presence of a wing dam just beneath the surface. And then again, the water may be nearly smooth over a slightly deeper wing dam.

There are two ramps, both without docks, on opposite sides of the river near mile 50.3. The marginal Montezuma Boat Landing sits on the RDB. Another useable ramp sits on the LDB in a trailer-park area. South of Montezuma at mile 48.6, the concrete Bedford Landing Boat Ramp is situated on the RDB. There is no public dock at this ramp, although there are many small private 15-foot docks in this area. You'll also see many elevated bungalows in this part of the river. There is another concrete ramp with no dock on the LDB at river mile 43.0, immediately south of the railroad bridge.

The enthralling little town of Kampsville, Illinois is at mile 32.1 on the RDB. A ferry crosses the river here. If the spare, and third, ferryboat is not being used, it may be tied off to the shore on the RDB just upriver from the actual ferry crossing. Recreational vessels are sometimes permitted to tie up overnight to this spare ferry and have access the town of Kampsville. If you do this, please clear your tie-up with the nearby ferry administration office. There are occasions when the ferry service will need to use this spare ferryboat. If that should happen, you would be required to unhitch from it on short notice.

Kampsville ferry, approaching the town

We arrived here just prior to Old Settler's Days in the third weekend in October. The festivities were a blast. Kampsville has two restaurants, an archeology museum, post office, convenience store, and year-round campground. The small museum, which is worth visiting, broadcasts Kampsville as the "Nile of North America," because of the many rich archeological finds in this area.

The Kampsville Ferry Area (618) 653-4518

Approach depth—8 feet
Accepts transients—yes (subject to ferryboat
    requirements)
Floating steel ferryboat—yes
Dockside water connections—nearby spigot
Boat ramp—yes
Restaurant—2 nearby

The river topography becomes interesting with sandstone bluffs, some as high as 120 feet, a distance away from the river. Alan Lloyd, author of *Great Circle Navigation Notes,* found and recommends an anchorage near mile 25.9 on the RDB. Alan says, "Round the southern tip of Hurricane Island and day-mark 25.9, then head north into Dark Chute behind Hurricane Island in 15 feet of water." (Parts or the entire set of *Great Circle Navigation Notes* can be ordered from Alan Lloyd, P.O. Box 217, Milford, OH 45150-0217 or e-mail Alloyd217@aol.com. Eight pages of notes cover the rivers in this guide.)

There are two floating 30-foot docks in six feet of water, and the seasonally opened Barefoot Bar, at mile 22.6 on the RDB. A narrow concrete ramp is to the north of the Barefoot Bar. A mile and a half south of the Barefoot Bar and south of the highway lift bridge, you'll find another great town. Hardin, Illinois is at mile 21.0 and also on the RDB.

Immediately south of the scenic river-frontage road in Hardin, you'll see a 250-foot-long dock belonging to the Illinois Riverdock Restaurant. There is about 10 feet of water off this dock, and the restaurant will permit you tie up gratis if you spend a little money in their restaurant. Fred praised the lemon meringue pie there. Besides being a great restaurant, the Riverdock offers a great selection of smoked meats.

Illinois Riverdock Restaurant (618) 576-2362

Approach depth—10 feet
Accepts transients—yes
Floating steel docks—yes
Boat ramp—nearby
Restaurant—on site and 2 nearby

There is a very nice public ramp area with a 60-foot floating dock and a picnic area south of the Riverdock Restaurant. The town of Hardin also has a convenience store, service station, post office, drugstore, and a couple of other restaurants. Mortland Island splits the river between miles 19.5 and 18.0. The Illinois River Channel is on the east, or LDB side, of the river. Joe and Betsey Butera found another anchorage for us near the south end of Mortland Island. South of mile marker 18.0, they entered the slough on the RDB side of the river behind the island. When entering this anchorage, Betsey and Joe found a shoal close to the RDB, but they did find deeper water on the Mortland Island side. They were able to anchor in 11-14 feet of water about a third of a mile from the main Illinois River Channel in this wide slough on the southwest side of Mortland Island.

There is a boat ramp with a small floating dock in another small slough on the LDB near mile 15.0. Another concrete boat ramp with

Kampsville ferry, and bluffs on the Illinois River

Old Settler's Days in Kampsville, on the Illinois River

Canoes and campfires at Old Settler's Days

Crafts at Old Settler's Days

Hardin municipal dock (foreground) and the Illinois Riverdock Restaurant dock

The boat launch area of Grafton

A Halloween-decorated house in Grafton

A Halloween-decorated front yard in Grafton

no dock is at mile 13.2 on the RDB. Pere Marquette State Park has a sizable harbor for shallow-draft vessels (i.e., less than four feet) on the LDB at mile 7.3. We found a tad deeper water in the channel entry slightly southeast of the channel's centerline. Inside, the harbor has about 40 boat slips. There have been long-standing plans to add greater amenities for boaters. The state park is one of Illinois's largest, with 8,000 acres and 12 miles of hiking trails. The visitor center explores Indian history, geology, and animal fossils; has exhibits on birds and flowers; and also has an aquarium containing Illinois River fish. Furthermore, the park has several picnic pavilions.

Pere Marquette State Park Boat Harbor
(618) 786-3323

Approach depth—4 feet
Accepts transients—yes
Floating wooden piers—yes
Boat ramp—yes
Restaurant—on site

For the past 30 miles, the Mississippi River has been paralleling the Illinois less than 10 miles away. Before the Illinois River spills into the Mississippi River, it gradually sweeps from a southerly to an easterly heading. The Brussels Ferry plies the Illinois River across river mile 3.7.

The pleasant town of Grafton, Illinois is situated between miles 0.0 and 1.0 on the LDB of the Illinois River. Grafton was founded by Marquette in 1673. There are two steel floating docks with four ramps near mile 0.4 on the LDB. The ramps are about 60 yards apart. There is about five feet of water off the longer easternmost dock.

Most of the town of Grafton is situated along the main river road and resembles a narrow ribbon. In Grafton you'll find a farmer's market, two wineries, several antique shops, the historic Ruebel Hotel, a few saloons, a post office, a convenience store, about four restaurants, and a fair number of bed-and-breakfast establishments. We were here in mid-October, and I cannot ever recollect a more tastefully decorated town for Halloween.

White chalk cliffs on the Mississippi downriver from Grafton, Illinois

CHAPTER 12

The Mississippi River, from Portage des Sioux, MO to Cairo, IL

The Mississippi River, for navigational purpose, is divided into two sections. The Lower Mississippi River includes the 855 miles between Cairo (pronounced KAY-ro), Illinois and New Orleans. There are no locks and dams slowing down the swift Mississippi on this lower portion. The Upper Mississippi River encompasses about 860 navigable miles between Minneapolis and Cairo. There are 25 locks and dams between Grafton, Illinois and Minneapolis. If you wish to learn about the Mississippi River marinas north of Grafton or south of Cairo, Illinois, refer to *Quimby's 2001 Cruising Guide.*

Before we arrived on the Mississippi River, we were often forewarned of its hazards. These foreboding reports have merit. The Mississippi today isn't as dangerous as it was in the 1830s, when the lifespan of a typical steamer was as short as 18 months. But there are very few services available for recreational boaters—probably fewer than a half-dozen facilities—on that entire 855-mile lower segment between Cairo and New Orleans. Commercial towboat traffic is intense, and the size of these tows is tremendous. We sometimes had morning fog on the Illinois River, but the morning fog on the Mississippi River was thicker and it hung around longer. The lower—farther south—one goes along the Mississippi River, the less suitable this river becomes for recreational boaters. Quimby's guide correctly states, "Mariners should carry a Road Atlas to locate themselves on this part of the river."

The Upper Mississippi River isn't nearly as dangerous nor difficult. But we are sailing on the lowest 217-mile section. Services and accommodations for recreational vessels are dwindling as we head south from Grafton to Cairo, Illinois. Nevertheless, the first 15 miles between Grafton and Alton, Illinois are loaded with recreational boating services amidst a scenic river background. There are spectacular white chalk cliffs for much of the way on the Illinois shore (i.e., the LDB). During the autumn, when we traveled, the colorful foliage of the hardwoods added to this ambiance.

On the Illinois River, shoreside daymarks were plentiful and easy to spot. But this is not the case on the Mississippi and Ohio rivers. We found only slightly more than half of the supposed 120 or so shoreside navigation aids on this 217-mile section of the Mississippi. We concluded that about one-quarter to one-fifth of those aids were no longer standing when we passed by their indicated locations on the Corps charts. We also discovered a few new standing aids that were not indicated on the charts. And we found about another 10 shoreside navigation aids near an aid that was marked on the chart but was a slight distance away. These particular aids displayed different mileage numbers than the ones shown on the Corps charts. It is likely these standing aids are newer, and better positioned for navigation, and the charts just haven't caught up with the latest navigational changes.

Unlike the Illinois River charts, the

Mississippi River charts show no floating aids (i.e., no can nor nun buoys). These buoys do exist, and they should be heeded. The Mississippi is such a turbulent and changing river, it likely makes little sense to "bed" these floating aids onto a chart. These floating aids sometimes get knocked far out of place by towboats. We noted several misplaced floating aids (e.g., a green can only a few feet away from the LDB, or a red nun only a few feet away from the RDB). Knowing that some floating aids may be way out of place, you should use common sense when assessing them. If you notice a buoy that appears out of place, it most probably *is* out of place.

Many times around curves in the river, there may be several floating aids of the same persuasion (e.g., all floating red nuns) closely packed. More so than normal, this should signal to you a sharp edge on that side of the channel. If you wish to keep water beneath your keel, you should appropriately honor all "sensible" floating aids, but especially those that are tightly packed together.

The Corps of Engineers charts also show many submerged wing dams and other features. These features are usually depicted in red on the Corps charts. The only marina professional that we were able to ask indicated that he never had heard of any boat striking a submerged wing dam.

The lower 217-mile section of the Mississippi River also has many rock jetties or dikes extending in to the river at an angle nearly perpendicular to the shore. You obviously want to avoid any encounter with these rock jetties. Nevertheless, they are reasonably accurately depicted on the Corps charts. On the charts, these narrow strips are shown in white and as thin extensions of the shore.

They are called "diversion dikes" and their purpose is interesting. Water flowing near the shore is diverted back to the center of the river by these dikes. This river water is artificially channeled to the center of the river and this fast-flowing water scours out the main channel, thus keeping it from silting. The diversion dikes have to be carefully positioned in order to maximize this scouring effect. I've been told similar-looking dikes on the Missouri River have a near opposite effect because the suspended solid load carried by the Missouri is quite different than that carried on the Mississippi River.

The downriver sides of many of these longer dikes make passable anchorages. We were able to obtain a comfortable anchoring depth behind almost every one of the longer dikes that we explored. Barring any other disconcerting features, we started approaching the shore at least 50 yards downriver from the tip of the dike. We then gradually turned upriver and worked our way in the lee of the rock dike. Once we were behind the protection of the dike we were also away from the strong current. We angled in toward the shore, away from the end of the dike, to a comfortable anchoring depth. Sometimes the water behind the dike was so calm that we even swung at anchor off the bow. For anchoring purposes, generally the farther out the dike protrudes into the Mississippi, the better. And the more surface water behind the dike, the better will be the anchorage. These features can be reasonably well ascertained from the Corps of Engineers charts. We've been told that the water level on the Mississippi River could vary as much as four feet, up or down, in the course of one night, so this is a consideration for overnight anchoring.

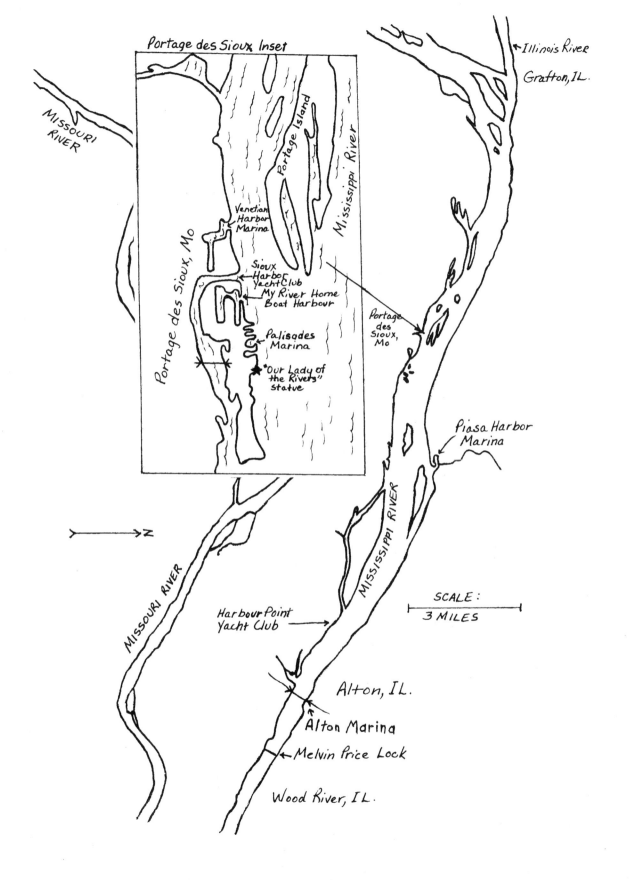

Portage des Sioux, Missouri is the first marina area downriver from the Illinois River mouth. Portage des Sioux is slightly more than five miles from Grafton and on the opposite side of the Mississippi River. This small town houses four marinas. It is best to leave the Mississippi River from the same point southeast of Portage Island to reach any of these four marinas. All of the marinas are south of, and at least slightly hidden by, Portage Island on the RDB. You can't miss the "Our Lady of the Rivers" statue. Approaching from upriver, near mile 212.5, upon seeing this statue, make a gradual turn toward the RDB and give the eastern tip of Portage Island searoom. Palisades Marina and Yacht Club is the first, and perhaps only, marina that can be seen from the river. It is also the one nearest to the statue. Approach Palisades Marina if you wish to visit any of the other three. The marinas are in the slough between Portage Island and the Missouri shore. The entry to Palisades Marina is fairly straightforward, but there is a protruding rock jetty as you near the marina. Our drawing depicts a 16-mile section of the Mississippi River between Grafton and Alton, Illinois. This particular drawing also has an inset for the marina area around Portage des Sioux.

My River Home Boat Harbour is the next marina upriver from Palisades Marina, and the entrance is marked by a Phillips 66 gas sign. This large powerboat marina has a single entry channel. The grounds at My River Home Boat Harbour are neatly maintained and the haul-out area is spacious. Sioux Harbor Yacht Club is the next facility upriver. Shaded Sioux Harbor also has a single entry, close to the entry of My River Home. Sioux Harbor caters to many sailboats. Venetian Harbor Marina is the fourth and most upriver marina in the Portage des Sioux area. The entry is a few hundred yards upriver from the entry to Sioux Harbor. Venetian Harbor, Sioux Harbor, and My River Home have approximately 150 slips. Palisades has about one-half as many. But both Palisades and Venetian Harbor have enough seawall to accommodate about a 200 footer. Venetian Harbor has the largest travel lift, the most yardwork character, and the best-stocked ship's store in the area. Palisades Marina was the only one of the four that we could reach on the VHF, as well as the only marina staffed during the Friday afternoon in October when we visited. Palisades Marina also has a pool and a nice restaurant. Covered docks prevail at all four of the facilities, and all four were close to full (i.e., transient space may be limited).

Palisades Marina and Yacht Club (636) 899-1093

Approach depth—5 feet
Accepts transients—yes
Floating wooden piers—yes
Dockside power connections—15 and 30 amp
Dockside water connections—yes
Showers—yes
Gasoline—yes
Diesel fuel—yes
Mechanical repairs—limited
Below-waterline repairs—yes
Boat ramp—yes
Restaurant—on site

My River Home Boat Harbour (636) 899-0903

Accepts transients—yes
Floating concrete docks—yes (all covered)
Dockside power connections—30 amp
Dockside water connections—yes
Showers—yes
Laundromat—yes
Gasoline—yes

Mechanical repairs—yes
Below-waterline repairs—yes
Boat ramp—yes
Ship's store—yes
Restaurant—on site

Sioux Harbor Yacht Club (636) 899-1634

Approach depth—8 feet
Accepts transients—yes
Floating steel and wooden docks—yes
Dockside power connections—20 and 30 amp
Dockside water connections—yes
Showers—yes
Gasoline—yes
Mechanical repairs—yes (independent
  contractor)
Below-waterline repairs—limited to 12-ton
  crane
Boat ramp—yes
Restaurant—several nearby

Venetian Harbor Marina (636) 899-0940

Approach depth—8 feet
Accepts transients—yes
Floating steel and wooden docks—yes
Dockside power connections—15, 30, and 50
  amp
Dockside water connections—yes
Showers—yes
Gasoline—yes
Diesel fuel—yes
Mechanical repairs—yes
Below-waterline repairs—yes
Ship's store—yes (large)
Restaurant—aboard towboat

The village of Portage des Sioux is within a fair walking distance from all four marinas. The town, as its name implies, was along the route of an Indian canoe portage trail connecting the Missouri and Mississippi rivers. This classic river town is more connected to the water than to neighboring towns. And it has often had to pay a terrible price for its

kinship with the Mississippi. When the Mississippi flooded horrifically in 1993, most of Portage des Sioux was under water. Every building in town sustained flood damage or worse, including all four of the marinas. The 50-foot Our Lady of the Rivers was mostly flooded. This shrine was built in gratitude after a horrific flood in 1951 stopped short of swallowing Portage des Sioux. If you're in the area on the third Sunday of July, you can catch the annual Blessing of the Fleet. The village of Portage des Sioux has a post office, a small food mart, and a church.

Two small boat harbors are located about a mile downriver from the Our Lady of the Rivers statue on the RDB near mile 211.4. It would be hard to maneuver in either harbor if your boat is over 25 feet.

Two small boat harbors

Approach depth—4 feet
Floating docks—yes
Below-waterline repairs—possibly with small
  cranes
Boat ramp—3 nearby

The main channel is closer to the Missouri shore (RDB) between miles 211 and 208. Eagles Nest Island and Piasa Island should be treated like the LDB in this area. Piasa Harbor Marina is behind Piasa Island on the LDB. The best approach to the marina is to depart the main Mississippi River channel near mile 207.2 and treat this island like the RDB (i.e., leave it to your south). Near mile 209.2, we were also able to wheedle our way by the western tip of Piasa Island. We rounded the eastern tip of Eagles Nest Island (and the duck blinds east of the island), and then we arced around the western tip of Piasa Island, staying as far as possible from both islands, before entering the secondary channel near the LDB and close to Piasa Harbor Marina. We encountered depth readings as low as four feet and we can't recommend this route to most of you. We recommend a more straightforward and better entry downriver. This entry would be the Piasa Harbor Marina channel—the one that departs the river near mile 207.2. In this downriver entry, we had over 30 feet of water much of the way, and never encountered less than 10 feet of water. When you approach Piasa Creek, the Piasa Harbor Light and Daymark is deceiving. Upon entering Piasa Creek, the red daymark is on the left side of the creek.

Much construction was taking place at Piasa Harbor and prospects appeared promising, with plans for a restaurant and nearby stores. When the construction is finished, this well-maintained marina will be have even more to offer. The marina should have around 275 slips and be capable of accommodating a 100 footer. Piasa Harbor sells diesel fuel and three grades of gasoline and has a pump-out station. This marina also has a docking area and fuel station on Piasa Creek, outside the main marina basin. This second outside area is particularly convenient for transient boaters who might prefer to minimize the uncertainty and the milling around that is often associated with "finding their way" in a strange marina basin. There are also four public boat launches across, on the east side of, Piasa Creek.

Piasa Harbor Marina (618) 466-7501

Approach depth—5 feet
Dockside depth—5 feet
Accepts transients—yes
Floating steel docks—yes

Dockside power connections—30 and 50 amp
Dockside water connections—yes
Waste pump-out—yes
Showers—yes
Gasoline—2 locations
Diesel fuel—2 locations
Mechanical repairs—yes
Below-waterline repairs—yes
Boat ramp—on site and many nearby
Ship's store—yes
Restaurant—under construction

The area around here is known as Piasa Country. The name comes from a legendary Indian dragonlike bird, the piasa bird. Marquette and Joliet saw this bird painted on a Mississippi River bluff as they canoed past it. Indian legend states that this great bird could carry a buck in its talons while in flight. But the mythical bird preferred human prey. After the piasa bird destroyed many Indian villages, it was finally slain by one brave and innovative chief and his band of warriors.

After Piasa Island, for about six miles, the main Mississippi channel favors the LDB. Harbour Point Yacht Club is across the river near mile 204.5. This is another large first-class facility, with about 225 slips and capable of accommodating a 75 footer. The orange and white Commodore Myer Light Tower sits downriver from the wide entry of Harbour Point Yacht Club. Furthermore, when departing, or taking a stern shot when entering, keep yourself in a line between the entry and the big blue tank ashore in the northern part of Alton, Illinois on the LDB. The heading to that blue tank should be about 85 degrees, or a back azimuth entry heading of 265 degrees.

Harbour Point Yacht Club (636) 899-1513

Approach depth—8 feet
Dockside depth—11 feet

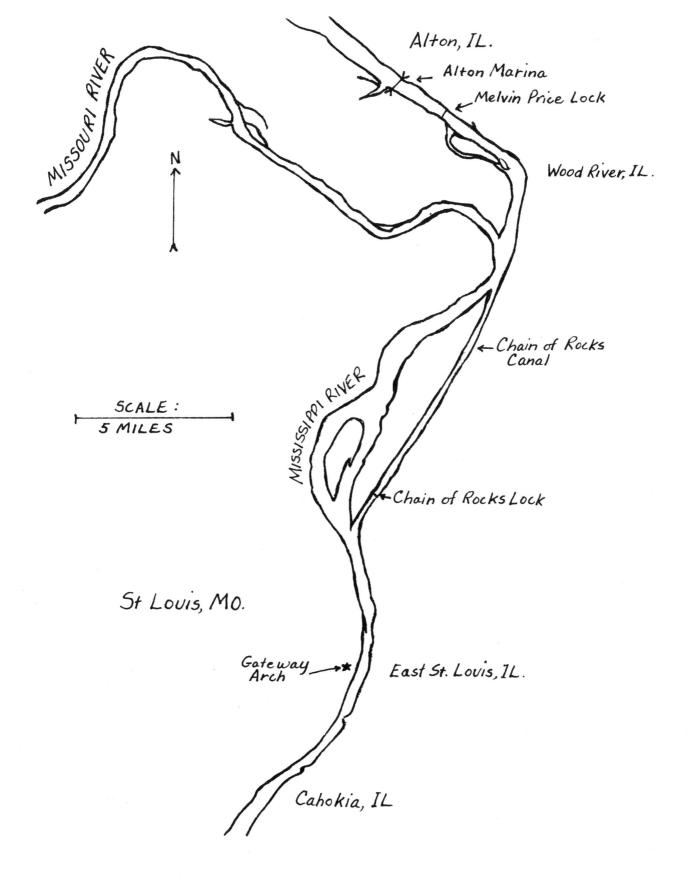

Accepts transients—yes
Floating concrete docks—yes
Dockside power connections—30 and 50 amp
Dockside water connections—yes
Showers—yes
Mechanical repairs—yes
Below-waterline repairs—yes

There were a few glaring, and potentially dangerous, inconsistencies between the Corps charts and the actual situation on the river. Lock and Dam 26 (the Melvin Price Lock and Dam) is not located at mile 202.9 as shown on the chart. The present lock and dam, completed in 1994, is farther downriver at mile 200.8. Today, the railroad drawbridge at Alton doesn't exist. At mile 194.2, the chart indicates taking a sailing line down the Mississippi River. This choice would prove to be disastrous. All boats should depart the Mississippi River on the LDB at mile 194.3 and use the Chain of Rocks Canal, bypassing a treacherous portion of the Mississippi River and another dam. Our drawing depicts a 30-mile section of the Mississippi River between Alton and Cahokia, Illinois, including the Chain of Rocks Canal. The following table lists the bridges, locks, ferries, and major river confluences covered in this chapter. The Corps charts do not indicate a vertical clearance for some of the first three bridges in this chapter. Nevertheless, it is believed that their vertical clearance is at least equal to the unimpeded vertical bridge clearances on the Lower Illinois River (i.e., 63 feet).

The two gaudy-colored Alton Belle Casino boats are at mile 203.2 on the LDB in Alton, Illinois. The photogenic, especially at night, William Clark Suspension Bridge crosses the river at mile 202.7. On the LDB, the entrance to Alton Marina is immediately downriver from the Clark Suspension Bridge. However, nearly all of the physical marina facility is situated on the upriver side of the bridge. There is a breakwater paralleling and downriver from the bridge. Enter the marina basin at the opening in the breakwater closer to the center of the river. The fuel dock is also just inside this breakwater. The 280-slip Alton Marina offers luxuries we haven't seen in a while, nor seen since. One particular amenity that I've never seen at a marina was a hot tub (actually there are two hot tubs). Besides their upscale marina amenities, such as a laundry, a pool, and private shower rooms, the entire marina floats. The marina is located about a third of a mile from the casino boats and downtown Alton. If you prefer not to walk, there is a regular marina shuttle service to the casino, the many downtown restaurants, and the grocery store.

Alton Marina (618) 462-9860
http://www.skipperbuds.com

Approach depth—12+ feet
Dockside depth—12+ feet
Accepts transients—yes
Floating wooden piers—yes
Dockside power connections—30 and 50 amp
Dockside water connections—yes
Waste pump-out—yes
Showers—yes
Laundromat—yes
Gasoline—yes
Diesel fuel—yes
Mechanical repairs—yes
Below-waterline repairs—limited
Boat ramp—yes
Ship's store and deli—yes
Restaurant—several nearby

Alton, Illinois was founded around river commerce in 1818. Across the river in St. Louis, abolitionist and newspaperman Elijay

BRIDGE NAME	TYPE	VERTICAL CLEARANCE (FEET)	APPROX RIVER MILE
		normal pool	
Confluence with Illinois River			218.0
U.S. 67 (William Clark Highway Bridge), Alton	Fixed	65	202.7
Melvin Price Lock and Dam (Lock and Dam 26)	Lock		200.8
Railroad bridge at Melvin Price Lock and Dam	Fixed	63	200.7
Confluence with Missouri River			195.0
North entrance to Chain of Rocks Canal			194.3
Chain of Rocks Road	Fixed	unknown	192.3
Interstate 270	Fixed	unknown	192.1
Chain of Rocks Lock (Lock and Dam 27)	Lock		185.5
South entrance to Chain of Rocks Canal			184.0
Merchants Railroad, St. Louis	Fixed	83	183.2
McKinley Highway and Railroad, St. Louis	Fixed	85	182.5
Martin Luther King Memorial, St. Louis	Fixed	96	180.2
Eads Highway and Railroad, St. Louis	Fixed	73	180.0
Interstates 55 & 70 (Poplar Street), St. Louis	Fixed	86	179.2
U.S. 460 (Douglas MacArthur Bridge)	Fixed	103	179.0
Interstate 255 & U.S. 50 (Jefferson Barracks)	Fixed	107	168.6
Ste. Genevieve Ferry	Ferry		125.3
Confluence with Kaskaskia River			117.5
Chester Highway, LDB span	Fixed	96	109.9
Cape Girardeau Highway	Fixed	105	51.6
Railroad, Thebes	Fixed	100	43.7
Interstate 57, center span, north of Cairo	Fixed	60	7.5
U.S. Routes 60 and 62, Cairo	Fixed	85	0.5
Confluence with Ohio River			0.0

Downtown Alton

Fred hanging with locals at El Carlito's Mexican Restaurant in Alton

Lovejoy was very effective in stirring up anti-slavery sentiment. In 1837, Lovejoy was railroaded out of St. Louis. Not to be silenced, he and his *Observer* newspaper relocated to nearby Alton. On November 7, 1837, his "fourth" printing press and he were attacked by another pro-slavery mob. Lovejoy was murdered, and his press was thrown into the Mississippi River. On October 15, 1858, the seventh, and final, Lincoln-Douglas debate was held in Alton. By most accounts, Lincoln lost the debate.

In the 1840s and 1850s, Alton was an important link in the Underground Railroad, whereby escaped slaves made their way north to freedom. Alton's proximity to the trading slave center of St. Louis coupled with its location in this "free state" along the Mississippi River made it an ideal spot for Underground Railroad activity. Illinois was flanked by slave states, and its natural borders with the meandering Mississippi and Ohio rivers also abetted the Underground Railroad. During the Civil War, Alton also housed a prisoner of war camp for captured Confederate soldiers. In the early 1860s, over 1,300 Confederate prisoners died of smallpox in this compound.

Today, besides Alton Marina and the casino boats, the city of Alton, Illinois has much to offer. It is the largest city on our trip since Peoria. Alton has a visitor center, grocery store, library, and many choices in fine restaurants. Fred and I enjoyed Alton so much that we took a leisurely half-day just to goof off. We spent a memorable evening in El Carlito's Mexican Restaurant mingling late at night with the hired hands, their family, and friends. El Carlito's brought back many fond memories of our Peace Corps days in Ecuador.

The Melvin Price Lock or Lock and Dam Number 26 is at mile 200.8. There are two parallel locking chambers on the LDB. This lock has the capability to place towboats in one pit (the larger chamber) and recreational boats in another, smaller, locking chamber closer to the Illinois shore. Melvin Price prefers VHF channel 14 and their phone number is (618) 462-1713. The lock uses eight floating bollards. You need to lasso a bollard with one of your own amidships dock lines in the recreational vessel chamber. The water level in the pit drops extremely fast—possibly twice as fast as the rate of most locks on the Illinois River. The forward section of this lock has less turbulence. The lift or drop is about 20 feet.

At Wood River, Illinois, near mile 198, the Mississippi bends about 90 degrees from an east-southeast direction to a south-southwest heading. In 1803, Wood River was the point of embarkation of the Lewis and Clark Expedition. Less than three miles downriver, the mighty Missouri River dumps into the Mississippi near mile 195. In times of high water, the Missouri River often dumps more volume of water into the Lower Mississippi River than the Upper Mississippi River branch does. It's the Missouri River, and not the Upper Mississippi River, that is more connected to the Lower Mississippi River. Today, the Missouri River is navigable for 733 miles, past Kansas City and on to Sioux City, Iowa. Of course, back in 1803, the Lewis and Clark Expedition took the Missouri River much farther, to about Yellowstone Park, before that momentous Corps of Discovery crossed our great divide on their way to the Pacific Coast.

About a mile south of the Missouri River, and on the LDB, the Chain of Rocks Canal departs the Mississippi River at mile 194.3.

All vessels should use the Chain of Rocks Canal. Do not navigate on the Mississippi River between miles 194 and 184. On the Mississippi River, there is a dam with no lock and the river is very treacherous here. The Chain of Rocks Canal is about nine miles long.

The Chain of Rocks Lock, or Lock 27, is about a mile from the southwestern entrance to this canal. Like the Melvin Price Lock, there are twin parallel locking chambers facilitating traffic movement through the lock. This lock prefers to communicate on VHF 12; it is too close to the Melvin Price Lock to be sharing the same VHF channel (i.e., VHF channel 14). The phone number of Lock 27, or the Chain of Rocks Lock, is (618) 452-7107. The north gate on the recreational lock at the Chain of Rocks rises or lowers staying perpendicular to the water level, instead of swinging open or closed. The drop or lift in this pit is about 12 feet.

About a mile downriver from the lock, the Chain of Rocks Canal reconnects to the Mississippi River. The Chain of Rocks Lock is the last lock on the Mississippi River. Downriver, and with the help of the scouring diversion dikes, the Mississippi will remain deep enough for barge traffic without the need for dams. And it will be descending fast.

South of the Chain of Rocks, the main Mississippi River channel is closer to the LDB than the RDB. This is slightly contrary to what is shown on the Corps chart. You are still about four miles north of downtown St. Louis and in a very industrialized area. South of the Chain of Rocks Canal, the river current picks up and the working river aspect intensifies. From here, and for the next 15 miles, the river will likely become chock-full of towboats. At mile 180.0, you'll go beneath the Eads Bridge, one of the first built to span the Mississippi River.

Upon reaching downtown St. Louis, Fred and I were planning to "sneak in" (i.e., park unobtrusively) our little 25 footer somewhere and sample the city's highlights, including a few of the many nightspots in Lacledes Landing. This riverfront landing is one of the oldest sections of St. Louis. In 1763, St. Louis was founded by Pierre Laclede and a French contingent coming from New Orleans. In the 1850s, the cobblestone streets and catacombs and caves in Lacledes Landing provided an ideal sallying location for the beginning of the northbound Underground Railroad. I have always had most memorable experiences when visiting this historic river city in the past.

But lo and behold, arriving by boat was a totally different and unhappy story. The *Tom Sawyer* and *Becky Thatcher* tour-boat docks had a handful of small out-of-the-way places where we could have fit and been out of their tour-boat traffic, at least for an hour or two. The dock custodian impertinently disallowed our request.

Alongside or behind, the closed-for-the-season *Robert E. Lee* paddlewheeler was another possibility. Again, there was a bit of tie-up space, but there was no way we could get through the locked gangway. We briefly tied to the floating McDonald's Restaurant near the base of the famed Gateway Arch. After our small inconspicuous boat was secured alongside the burger joint, we went inside and ordered a meal. Before I could finish my Big Mac, the manager came out and ordered us to leave. I found it most disheartening that this wonderful city, established by river commerce and with such

St. Louis Gateway Arch

fabulous historical river roots, does not have even meager accommodations nor hospitality for the boaters of today. The nearest recreational boating facilities to the riverfront of St. Louis are either at Alton Marina, 23 miles to the north, or Hoppie's Marina, 20 miles to the south.

South of St. Louis, both sides of the river continue to be clogged with barges. You need a heightened state of attention in this area because there is much towboat activity. There is a U.S. Coast Guard Station in St. Louis, and the phone number is (314) 539-3706.

Our drawing depicts about an 80-mile section of the Mississippi River between Cahokia and Chester, Illinois. The Jefferson Barracks Bridge, carrying Interstate 255 and U.S. Route 50, crosses the river near mile 169. Barge activity begins to thin out slightly south of this bridge.

Hoppie's Marina is 10 miles south of the Jefferson Barracks Bridge on the RDB, outside of Kimmswick, Missouri near river mile 158.3. Hoppie's Marina was likely the most salt-of-the-earth place on our entire trip. Husband-and-wife team Capt. Charles and Fern Hopkins, along with their daughter, precisely help guide transient boaters to a safe harborage and away from the turbulent current. Their marina isn't much more than a few barges

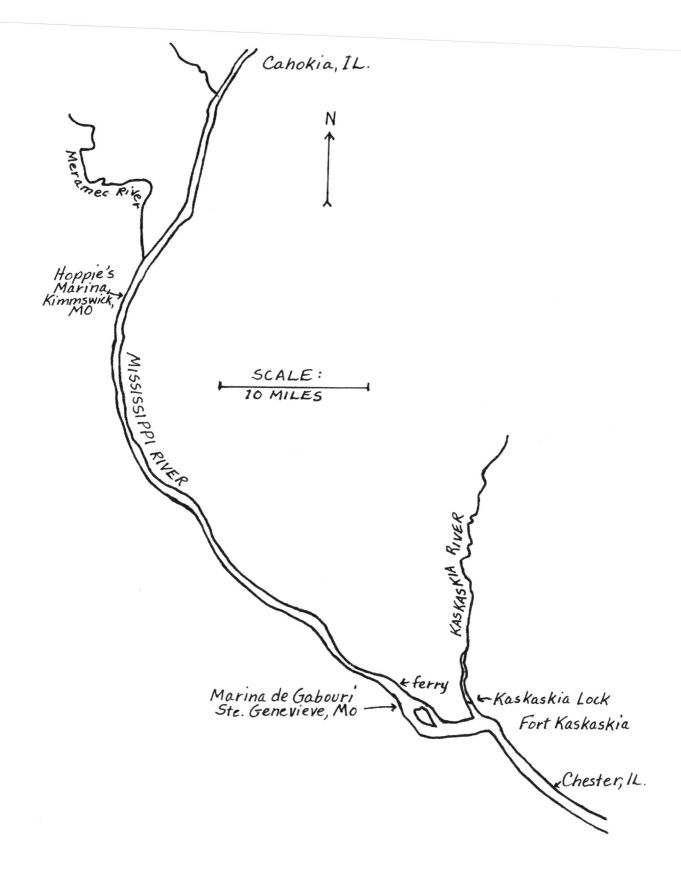

Hoppie's Marina, with a barge in the background

Fern Hopkins, center, overseeing things at Hoppie's Marina

Hoppie's Marina social plaza

moored parallel to the RDB. Nonetheless, it's a most welcoming place. All docking is side-tie on the river. There is about 300 feet of docking space parallel to the river on each side of the barges. The Hopkinses are perhaps the most knowledgeable people on the river we encountered. They lived through storms and 40-foot floods and have "seen it all" from us tenderfoot transient boaters. If the river level is low, the next marina, Marina de Gabouri, may be totally inaccessible. If so, Hoppie's may be the last place to easily purchase gasoline or diesel for the next 205 miles.

Hoppie's Marina (636) 467-6154

Approach depth—12 feet

Dockside depth—12 feet
Accepts transients—yes, reservations appreciated
Floating steel docks—yes
Dockside power connections—30 and 50 amp
Dockside water connections—yes
Gasoline—yes
Diesel fuel—yes
Mechanical repairs—limited
Boat ramp—yes
Restaurant—2 about a mile away in Kimmswick

The village of Kimmswick, Missouri is about a mile north of and accessible from Hoppie's. Like Hoppie's, Kimmswick is a colorful town with rich river history and lore. The town was laid out in 1859 to take advantage of the river and rail traffic. Kimmswick prospered after the

Civil War. But later, the automobile and the highways bypassed the town. Kimmswick has two nice restaurants, two small grocers, and a few bed and breakfast places.

There is not much on the remainder of the Upper Mississippi River for us recreational boaters. There are a few scattered boat ramps, and very few have docks. We observed about a 35-foot dock near mile 150 on the RDB. Crystal City, Missouri sits about a mile west of this dock and ramp. The next dock is about 100 miles downriver at Honker's Boat Club in Cape Girardeau, Missouri. Power lines cross the river near mile 148. A boat ramp, without a dock, was observed near mile 140.5 on the RDB. A ferryboat plies the Mississippi near mile 125.5.

You might notice Gabouri Creek at Mississippi River mile 122.5 on the RDB. And then again Gabouri Creek might be dried up. The town of Ste. Genevieve, Missouri is about two miles west along this creek bed. There is a marina a hundred yards or so up Gabouri Creek. We were unable to visit this marina in mid-October 2000, because the creek was totally dry. When we telephoned the marina we were informed that the marina facilities close down when the river level gets low. This usually doesn't happen until after Labor Day. But it could happen as early as August, as it did in 2000.

Marina de Gabouri (573) 883-5509

Approach depth—dry and unapproachable in Oct. 2000
Accepts transients—yes
Dockside power connections—30 and 50 amp
Dockside water connections—yes
Showers—yes
Gasoline—yes
Diesel fuel—yes
Restaurant—on site

On the LDB, don't confuse the two sloughs at miles 122 and 120 on the LDB with the Kaskaskia River. The real Kaskaskia River enters the Mississippi at mile 117.5 on the LDB. The Kaskaskia Lock and Dam is four-fifths of a mile up the Kaskaskia River and off the Mississippi River. The Kaskaskia Lock is on the RDB of the Kaskaskia River. Recreational boats can tie up overnight to the lock's guide wall, which is over 600 feet long. But boaters are not allowed to get off of their boat while tied up. Please contact the Kaskaskia Lock tender for further instructions. The lock tender monitors VHF 16 and 14. There are also a few boat ramps in the Kaskaskia River. There is a double ramp near the upriver end of the lock and another ramp in the downriver end of the lock.

About 300 years ago, Kaskaskia was primarily populated by the French, and it was one of the biggest towns in the "West." The "Kaskaskia" name was transported from a tribe of Indians who once roamed along the Illinois River near Ottawa during Marquette's time. About 230 years ago, there was a British fort at Kaskaskia. On the night of July 4, 1778, the British, in a war with a fledgling nation, were expecting an American attack via the Mississippi River. George Rogers Clark and his men from Virginia surprised the British by marching overland through Illinois. Clark captured the British fort without resistance. Later, Clark marched north along the Mississippi River and also secured the British fort at Cahokia, Illinois. In 1790, Kaskaskia was the seat of government for America's "Northwest Territory."

Another boat ramp was observed on the RDB at Mississippi River mile 115.5. A highway bridge crosses the river at Chester, Illinois near river mile 110. There are two boat ramps

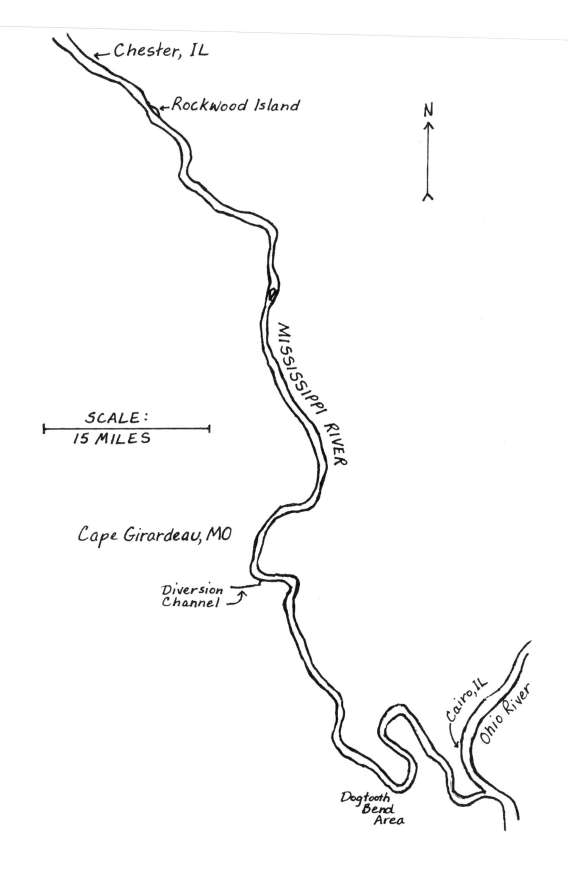

Chester, IL

Rockwood Island

N

MISSISSIPPI RIVER

SCALE:
15 MILES

Cape Girardeau, MO

Diversion
Channel

Cairo, IL

Ohio River

Dogtooth
Bend
Area

on the LDB, one on each side of the highway bridge. Typically, neither ramps had a dock. Hence, we had no access to the town of Chester from either the LDB or the RDB. Like Alton upriver, Chester was another important link in the Underground Railroad.

Our next drawing depicts the lowest 110-mile section of the Upper Mississippi River, from Chester to Cairo, Illinois. We did find a suitable overnight anchorage behind the dike on the LDB at mile 102.4. This anchorage is only about 70 yards northwest of Rockwood Island. From about 80 yards downriver from the tip of the dike, we turned north-northeast (i.e., about a 15-degree heading) toward Rockwood Island. Once in the lee of the dike, we stayed 20 yards off Rockwood Island and approached the anchorage from the south. We found 8-14 feet of water and a muddy bottom, and we even swung a bit at anchor in this relatively calm pool.

After Rockwood Island, the Mississippi River floodplain gradually shifts from the RDB to the LDB. This lower topography on the LDB will hold for about 65 miles. Near Cape Girardeau, the river bluffs fade into a wide alluvial valley. This was the long-ago reach of the ancient Gulf of Mexico.

In a bend near mile 94, we encountered a few whirlpools, back eddies, and unusual turbulence. River depths changed abruptly from about 25 feet to over 60 feet. Our boat speed-dogged down, and we lost some boat control. We're glad we didn't encounter a towboat in this bend.

Near mile 80 on the RDB, you'll see the Tower Rock limestone formation. Native Americans believed that this unusual rock outcrop in the river was the domain of evil spirits because Indian canoes were sometimes destroyed by the currents and the rocks. There is a boat ramp on the LDB slightly downriver from Tower Rock.

Cape Girardeau, Missouri, between miles 53 and 51 on the RDB, is a most pleasant river town. But it has the same problem nearly all of these Mississippi River towns have—it is virtually inaccessible to recreational boaters. There are a few questionable short-term tie-up potentials in the area. Honker's Boat Club has a 70-foot floating dock and a ramp at mile 53 on the RDB. The small club is private, their dock isn't well secured, and they are, at best, hesitant about transient boaters tying up. Kidd's 50-foot Fuel Dock is at mile 51.9 on the RDB. Overnight tying up is prohibited at Kidd's even if you buy fuel. This is a mobile fueling operation working off a tanker truck. You are required to call Kidd's 24 hours in advance, and once again one hour before arriving. You also need to purchase no less than 50 gallons of fuel. Kidd's would have no problem with multiple boats getting together to make that "50-gallon limit" at one filling. Kidd's working hours are from 8:00 A.M. to 5:00 P.M. You probably could get fuel on the weekend, if you paid an additional $15 premium. We chanced upon another source of portable fuel around Cape Girardeau. Steve Perkins, of Eagle Oil Company, also operates a tanker truck. He has taken that truck out to fuel boats at Honker's, or to anywhere else where a boat could nose close to a road on shore. Like Kidd's, Steve probably needs a minimum purchase in order to make his trip worthwhile, and he appreciates any advance notification. Steve's phone numbers are (573) 243-1449 (Eagle Oil) and (573) 339-1726 (residence).

Cape Girardeau

Honker's Boat Club

Approach depth—7 feet
Accepts transients—no
Floating steel dock—yes
Boat ramp—yes

Kidd's Fuel Dock (573) 335-8160

Approach depth—10 feet
Accepts transients—no

Floating steel service dock—yes
Gasoline—yes
Diesel fuel—yes

At the base of downtown Cape Girardeau there is a rock floodwall at the river's edge. We saw a 40 footer attempting to tie up here. It was ugly. There was nothing onto which they could hook their lines, and there were rocks close to their boat in shallow water.

They soon smartly gave up, but then they snagged a river buoy working their way back to the channel.

We have heard of boats anchoring across the river in the protection of one of the diversion dikes on the LDB. Leaving a boat at anchor behind the dike, a boater could access Cape Girardeau via dinghy—and a dink with some horsepower (i.e., no rowing dinghy) in this current. After arriving at that rock floodwall, you would need to find a way to secure the dink with a long painter or two. If you had the spunk and ingenuity to visit Cape Girardeau by water, you'd find the historic riverfront district and a grocery store. Cape Girardeau is a very nice town, but just possibly too difficult and too dangerous to access for a recreational vessel.

A new highway bridge was being constructed next to the old bridge on the south side of Cape Girardeau. One of the better anchorages on this part of the Mississippi is about two miles south of this Cape Girardeau Bridge at mile 48.8 on the RDB. The narrow Little River Diversion Channel extends from the east to the west for dozens of miles. The canal remains comfortably deep up to the bridge over the canal and even well beyond this bridge. Betsey Butera informed me that this canal was designed by the same individual who designed the Panama Canal. The canal was built to divert the runoff from land to the north. Without the canal, the fertile farmland to the south of the canal would be threatened by northern runoff. The night when we were inside the mouth of this diversion channel, a couple of large (i.e., four feet long) mammals (river otters?) were making one heck of a nighttime ruckus splashing around our boat.

A railroad bridge crosses the river at Thebes, Illinois at mile 43.7. Just before this bridge, there is a nice boat ramp, with no dock, at mile 43.9 LDB. A potential anchorage looked good on the Corps of Engineers chart at mile 35.3 on the LDB, east of Burnham Island. We tried to enter, but we didn't like it. We were reading only four-foot depths in stiff current, and we were still 40 yards from the LDB.

The Dogtooth Bend Area of the Mississippi starts 25 river miles before Cairo, but entering this S bend, you are only about eight miles from Cairo as the crow flies. Cairo is a huge area for towboat staging and traffic. Even though you may be 25 river miles from the junction of the Ohio River, the VHF radio waves will be overloaded with towboat traffic from Dogtooth Bend and well into the Ohio River.

Downriver from Greenleaf Bend (the fourth bend in the Dogtooth Bend series), there are two anchorage areas accessible to recreational boaters. The first, and lesser known, anchorage is just north of the interstate highway bridge, near river mile 7.6 on the LDB. There is a partially submerged rock wall southeast of Boston Bar Island. To enter this anchorage, go to a point about 150 yards upriver from the bridge. Respect the red channel buoy north of the bridge. From a point near the buoy, take a heading of about 335 degrees to the center of the anchorage, leaving that partially submerged rock wall to your port, and west, as you enter. You should encounter about 11 feet of water most of the way into this anchorage. Near the head of the anchorage basin, we

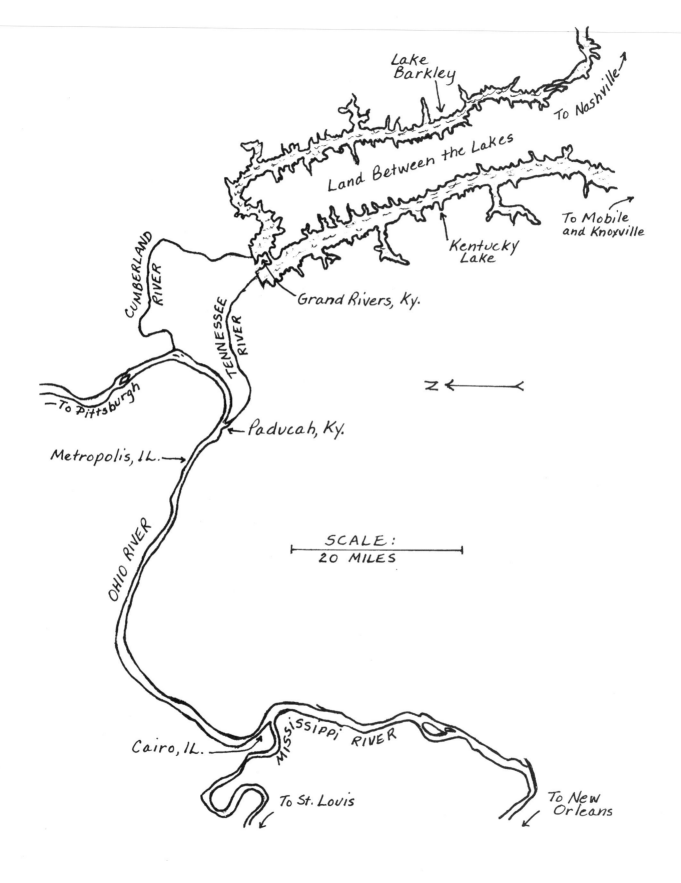

Lake Barkley

To Nashville

Land Between the Lakes

To Mobile and Knoxville

Kentucky Lake

CUMBERLAND RIVER

TENNESSEE RIVER

Grand Rivers, Ky.

N

To Pittsburgh

Paducah, Ky.

Metropolis, IL.

OHIO RIVER

SCALE: 20 MILES

Cairo, IL.

MISSISSIPPI RIVER

To St. Louis

To New Orleans

found five feet of water about 20 yards from the sandy shore.

There is another anchorage six miles downriver, a little more than two miles past Greenfield Bend. This Angelo Towhead Island anchorage is at mile 1.4 on the LDB, and just upstream from the U.S. highway bridge. This anchorage has a wider entrance than the Boston Bar anchorage. We entered the anchorage on a heading of 275 degrees. The deeper water, around 10 feet in depth, is more on the Angelo Towhead side of the anchorage. Less than a 10th of a mile into the slough, we encountered only four feet of water about 40 yards away from the LDB (i.e., the side opposite of Angelo Towhead). There were also more than a few protruding displaced trees and stumps scattered around this anchorage.

The Mississippi River joins the Ohio River downriver from the Cairo Bridge. The controlling channel depth of the Mississippi River will increase from nine to 12 feet south of Cairo. If you stay on the deeper Mississippi, it's 855 miles to New Orleans. Good luck. If you turn left, or northwest up the Ohio River, it could be only about another 711 miles to Mobile. The Mobile route is much safer and has hundreds more options for recreational vessels. Our drawing here displays portions of the Mississippi, Ohio, lower Cumberland, and lower Tennessee rivers, and Western Kentucky. From this "four river" area, we have many choice river destinations—Mobile, Knoxville, Nashville, Louisville, Cincinnati, Pittsburgh, and even New Orleans.

Barge traffic near Cairo

CHAPTER 13

The Foot of the Ohio River, to the Smithland Lock and Dam

As we turn east, or left and upriver, on the Ohio River, the LDB (left descending bank) switches sides. The LDB has been on our left for more than 500 miles, since Chicago (or perhaps Minneapolis). But once we turn *up* the Ohio, the Ohio LDB will now be on our *right* (or starboard) side. And the RDB (right descending bank) of the Ohio will be on our left, or port, side. This upriver convention will remain, as we continue to go upriver on either the Cumberland or the Tennessee rivers. If you plan to take the Tennessee River to the Tombigbee Waterway, the convention will switch again, as you start to go "downhill" after Pickwick Landing Lake and Yellow Creek. If you continued on this route, you would descend the 12 locks of the Tenn-Tom Waterway through Mississippi and Alabama. Please revisit the second diagram in chapter 3.

We found that the correlation between shoreside daymarks on the Corps of Engineers charts and their location on the Ohio River was much better than what we experienced on the Mississippi River. The Ohio River Corps charts also depicted floating can and nun buoys, and the chart correlation with the actual floating buoy locations is reasonably accurate.

The Ohio, along with the Missouri, is one of biggest tributaries of the Mississippi River. Four years before the Marquette and Joliet expedition, our familiar Frenchman, La Salle, was the first European to "discover" the upper reaches of the Ohio River, in the year 1669. As you round the junction daymark at Cairo Point and Fort Defiance State Park, you are heading up the bluer Ohio River. Gen. Ulysses S. Grant once commanded at Fort Defiance. His thrust southward was launched from Cairo, Illinois. Cairo is at the confluence of the Ohio and Mississippi rivers and on the RDB of the Ohio.

Our drawing depicts the lowest 60-mile section of the Ohio River. You may experience a slightly adverse current on the Ohio. We estimated that the current was between one and a half and two and a half knots. This is considerably less than the four-plus-knot current that was helping us down the Mississippi.

Two bridges span the river and their roads rim the town of Cairo. We found no access for a recreational boat to the town of Cairo, nor to the next two towns upriver on the RDB—Future City and Mound City, Illinois. Nevertheless, we did see two boat ramps on the RDB. But neither ramp had a dock. The first nice concrete ramp is at mile 980.8, at Fort Defiance State Park. The second ramp is at mile 979.2, below the Cairo floodwall.

The following table lists the bridges, locks, and major river confluences covered in this chapter.

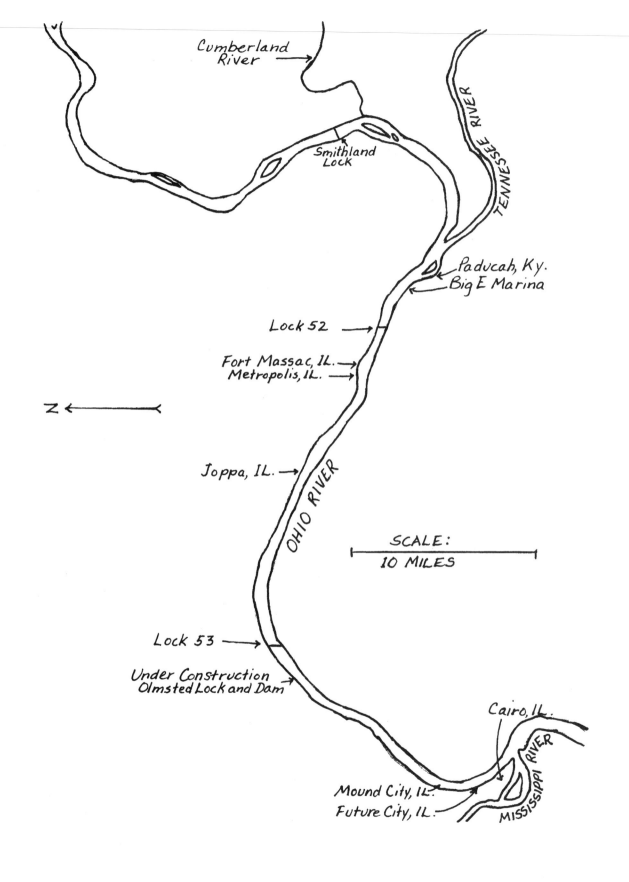

BRIDGE NAME	TYPE	VERTICAL CLEARANCE (FEET)	APPROX RIVER MILE
		normal pool	
Confluence with Mississippi River			981.5
U.S. Routes 51, 60, 62, Cairo	Fixed	105	980.4
Illinois Central Railroad	Fixed	104	977.7
Olmsted Lock and Dam (under construction)			964.7
Lock and Dam 53	Lock		962.6
P & I Railroad	Fixed	98	944.1
Interstate 24, Metropolis	Fixed	75	940.9
Lock and Dam 52	Lock		939.0
U.S. Route 45, Brookport-Paducah	Fixed	91	937.3
Confluence with Tennessee River, Paducah			934.5
Confluence with Tennessee River, Owens Island, East			932.8
Confluence with Cumberland River, Smithland			923.0
Smithland Lock and Dam	Lock		918.7

Besides having no good access to the town of Cairo, the entire Ohio River in front of Cairo is an extremely busy staging area for towboats. There are many tows going up, down, and across the river. And there are also many barges on moorings in the middle of the river. These barge-mooring areas are roughly depicted on the Corps of Engineers charts. Nevertheless, you can't relax at the helm here. The Ohio River is bustling with this towboat activity for its lowest nine miles. But the activity decreases northeast of Mound City. There are two more boat ramps, both without docks, near Mound City on the RDB. An unimproved ramp is at mile 974. A much larger concrete double ramp, with an ample parking area, is at mile 973. Mound City, like Cairo and Cape Girardeau to a lesser extent, is almost totally hidden behind a levee. North of Mound City, the Ohio becomes an easygoing river. At

Olmsted Landing, about 400 yards downriver from the construction site, at mile 965 on the RDB, there is another concrete boat ramp without a dock.

The two locks and dams near the foot of the Ohio River are old locks. They have a bit more turbulence than other locks because they have a limited number of large valves. The newer locks use more but smaller valves to dissipate the water flow in the lock. Lock and Dam 53 and Lock and Dam 52 are both being replaced by one new lock and dam—the Olmsted Lock and Dam. This is under construction near mile 964.7. This lock and dam is still years away from completion. Nevertheless, its construction is well under way. We noted that there were nine cranes operating on the RDB. This RDB side will house the lock. I was told that much of the dam is being cast upriver near Paducah, Kentucky. When the parts of the dam are ready, large pieces will be floated down from Paducah and sunk into position near Olmsted. Supposedly, all of the 53 "old dams" on the Ohio River will be replaced by about 19 "newer dams" similar to the Olmsted Lock and Dam.

Lock and Dam 53, built in 1929, is at mile 962.6. The lock is on the RDB and channel side of the Ohio River. The drop or lift at this dam may vary substantially—from 0 to 10 feet.

When we passed through, the dam was actually down and lowered into the river bed. The area was "open river" and the lock was bypassed. Nevertheless, there was a stronger than normal current—close to three extra knots—over this constriction in the river where a portion of the dam was lowered.

If the dam were up, naturally we would have locked. We would have thrown a line from our vessel to the lock tender. He would have looped that line around a check pin, and then sent our line back down to our vessel. Lock 53 monitors VHF 13 and 14 and can be reached at phone (618) 742-6213.

Joe and Betsey Butera hailed the lock tender on the VHF radio and obtained permission to tie up overnight to a safe place on the upriver end of the lockwall. If you even contemplate doing something like this, please obtain permission from the lock tender, as Joe and Betsey had done. Near universally, lock tenders will try to accommodate you if they can and keep you out of harm's way. I've also found that the lock tenders are the best reservoir of local river knowledge. If they are not too busy, and you treat them professionally and respectfully, they can be a great aid to an "unschooled on local knowledge" recreational boater.

There are two ramps between miles 958 and 956. One is near mile 958 on the RDB and in a campground area. The other is near mile 956 on the LDB—and our first ramp in Kentucky. Neither of these ramps has docks. What good are all of these small boat ramp locations to a large cruising trawler or sailboat? Probably not much, besides serving as river landmarks. Nevertheless, a ramp, with or without a dock, leads to a road; and a road sooner or later leads to a town . . . and to goods and services.

On the Ohio River, we couldn't safely land our vessel in Cairo, Future City, nor Mound City, but we did find a spot at Joppa, Illinois. The tie-up near Joppa is tricky and we would not recommend it when the river has any chop. Somewhere near river mile 951.4, and less than a half-mile after the easternmost power-line crossing, you should see an old railroad bed falling off into the river on the RDB. We approached this rail bed and found 5 feet of water at the shoreline and near the deepest—the downriver—end of this old railhead. We tied off to some half-rotten wooden railroad pilings and were able to get ashore while keeping our feet dry. If you walk about a quarter of a mile upriver along the beach, you come to a double concrete ramp area. Turn perpendicular to the shore, along the paved road. The little village of Joppa is about another third of a mile on the paved road. Joppa has a convenience store, with limited groceries, and a pizza place. After our many miles and days on the Mississippi River, Joppa was our first real "landfall." Despite its limited amenities, we had a blast there.

If it's impractical, or the river is too rough, to make that tricky landfall near Joppa, the larger town of Metropolis, Illinois is only another nine

At the old Joppa railhead

Metropolis and the *U*-shaped dock, with a barge in the background

miles up the Ohio River. After the Metropolis railroad bridge and just downriver from the Player's Island Casino Boat, there are two more ramps, without docks, near mile 944 on the RDB. There is also another boat ramp across the river in Kentucky.

Metropolis is much larger than Joppa. The very-visible Metropolis water tower is decorated with a Superman painting. Of course . . . Superman lived in Metropolis.

The best access to Metropolis is on the east end of town where there is a wide concrete ramp, near river mile 942.2 on the RDB. A U-shaped floating dock is near this ramp. The docks are about 20 feet in length, but a 25 to 30 footer can attach itself reasonably well. The water depth off the dock is about five feet. Our friends Joe and Betsey Butera stayed in Metropolis for three days. They found two different anchorages—one on each side of the dock, close to shore, and out of the channel. The ramp and dock area is at the foot of Fort Massac State Park.

In 1757, Fort Massac was built by French colonists as a trading center and an outpost to defend against the British. Around 1763, following the French and Indian War, the French ceded all of this area, known as the Northwest Territory, to the British. In 1778, Virginia governor Patrick Henry sent George Rogers Clark on a bold and far-reaching military mission to wrest our young nation's "western frontier" from British control. Clark and about 175 Virginians, who were known as the Long Knives, departed from Fort Pitt (present-day Pittsburgh) at the confluence of the Allegheny and Monongahela rivers in mid-May. They then sailed down the Ohio River. Upon their arrival at Fort Massac in late June, the Long Knives found the British fort abandoned. With

no resistance, Clark and his men entered Illinois. The British at Kaskaskia were expecting an American attack from the Mississippi River and they had scouts along the rivers. Clark, aware of this, marched his Long Knives overland and in single file to Kaskaskia. Catching the British off guard, Clark easily secured the old French capital and British fort at Kaskaskia on July 4, 1778.

Clark then marched 60 miles up along the Mississippi River and captured the British fort at Cahokia. His biggest prize, likely making him the most celebrated Revolutionary War hero of the "west," was yet to come. After Cahokia, 200 miles to the northeast, Clark soon secured the British stronghold at Vincennes on the Wabash River.

In 1794, the Americans rebuilt and garrisoned Fort Massac to protect our young nation's interest along the lower Ohio River. In the 1790s, the Spanish controlled the land west of the Mississippi River. In 1796, the Spanish sent the galley *Rays* up the Ohio River to test the Americans' resolve. The *Rays* was propelled by sails and 24 enslaved oarsmen, and she carried a company of soldiers. American captain Zebulon Pike, later to become more famous out west, had his men fire a six-round cannon across her bow. The *Rays* was forced ashore and Captain Pike ordered the Spaniards "out of American waters." On their historic trip, Lewis and Clark stopped by Fort Massac to procure some supplies and supplement their manning. In 1814, after the War of 1812, the fort was no longer needed and abandoned once again.

Native American history in this area is very rich. Tribes from the Shawnee and Miami Indians, both original residents of Ohio, migrated west along the Ohio River to the Fort Massac area. In 1908, Fort Massac was dedicated as Illinois's first state park. We visited Fort Massac, just before the "The Encampment" weekend in October. There was quite a three-day festival brewing—colonial crafting, reenactments, bagpipes, fifes and drums, river lore exhibits, and firework displays at night.

The road outside of Fort Massac State Park is about a third of a mile from the boat ramp. To the north, on this road, you'll find several restaurants (mostly fast food) and a Days Inn. In the opposite direction, toward the center of Metropolis, you'll find a grocery store, laundromat, drugstore, and several more fast-food restaurants. Metropolis is the first "small boat" accessible town since Kimmswick, Missouri, 200 miles ago.

Lock and Dam 52, at mile 939.0, is much like Lock and Dam 53. The lock tender monitors VHF 13 and 14 and can be reached at (618) 564-3151. After you arrive in the recreational vessel locking pit, you should throw a line from your vessel to the lock tender. After looping that line through a check pin, the lock tender throws that same line back down to you. There was open water at Lock 53, but 24 miles upriver, we encountered about a 12-foot lift at Lock 52.

"The Encampment" at Fort Massac

Near Brookport, Illinois, we observed another concrete boat ramp without a dock at mile 938 on the RDB. The U.S. Route 45 Bridge connects Paducah, Kentucky to Brookport, Illinois. Big E Marina is the first accessible bona-fide marina (i.e., with fuel and transient slips) since Hoppie's Marina, 205 miles ago. But neither Big E nor Hoppie's have showers. Big E juts out into the Ohio River and is hinged to the large motel complex west of Paducah, the Executive Inn. Like Hoppie's, it's a small marina, but nonetheless a most welcome find. Big E has about 20 slips and the facility could accommodate about a 100 footer. A room for the night at the adjoining Executive Inn would include the use of a pool and exercise room.

Big E Marina (270) 442-8200

Approach depth—11 feet
Accepts transients—yes
Floating steel docks—yes
Dockside power connections—no
Dockside water connections—yes
Laundromat—nearby
Gasoline—yes
Diesel fuel—yes
**Restaurant—in the Executive Inn and
   several nearby**

Historical downtown Paducah can also be accessed from the large floating steel platform at mile 934.5 on the LDB. This large platform is sometimes used by fishermen. It is connected by a gangway to the colossal Paducah

Betsey and Fred on the Paducah dock

The tastefully painted floodwall in Paducah

The steam locomotive on the Paducah waterfront

Fred at the Center for Maritime Education in Paducah

Municipal Launch Area. A most tastefully decorated floodwall mural, depicting scenes from Paducah's historic past, is situated up on the hill from the ramp. An old steam locomotive sits beyond the wall on Water Street. The River Heritage Museum, (270) 575-9958, and the Center for Maritime Education are less than a block away. Capt. Jerry Tinkey, (270) 575-1005, provided us with an excellent tour of the latter. Fourteen of the largest barge companies regularly send their crews here for the excellent ongoing professional training in various aspects of seamanship. The center has four interactive pilothouse simulators. It was extremely heartening to learn of all the

serious training, and retraining, taking place at this facility.

City of Paducah Broadway Wharf Municipal Launch Area

Approach depth—12 feet
Accepts transients—yes (a sign says limited to 30 minutes)
Floating steel platform—yes
Restaurant—several nearby

The Chickasaw Indians inhabited this area before the white man. In 1795, Revolutionary War hero George Rogers Clark laid claim to a disputed 37,000 acres near the mouth of the Tennessee River. After Clark died, the U.S.

Supreme Court later ruled in his favor. In 1827, his younger brother William Clark (of the famed Lewis and Clark Expedition) gained the deed. William Clark platted a town, and either named it after the Padouca Indians or their legendary and peaceful chief, Chief Paduke. Paducah boasts of producing statesman Alben Barkley and humorist Irvin Cobb in the past century. For the last 100 years, Paducah has also been an important barge-building and -repair center. To this day, "river-related industries" are crucial to the Paducah economy. All of the commercial traffic coming from upriver—out of the 930 navigable miles of the Ohio River, or the 650 miles of the Tennessee River, or even the 390 naviga-

ble miles of the Cumberland River—has to pass by Paducah's front porch. Furthermore, in the wintertime, Paducah is the northernmost ice-free city along this system of rivers.

Within six blocks of the Ohio River, Paducah has a hardware store, a library, a convenience store, a few upscale restaurants. The Greyhound Bus station and a liquor store are a few blocks farther from the river. After a "hard day" on these heartland rivers, and after the hook is down or you're tied to a dock, you may, or may not, be entitled to a drink. If you regularly restock your vessel with Class IV goods (i.e., liquor), and you are heading south, it is advised that you stock up in Paducah. It may be nearly 450 miles, and well

Downtown Paducah

into Alabama, before you can buy liquor again. The upcoming counties south in Kentucky, Tennessee, and Mississippi along the "Great Circle" are "dry counties."

Paducah has several informative attractions, including the Market House and a railroad museum. The Museum of the American Quilter's Society attracts visitors from around the world. The museum has three galleries.

From Paducah, heading toward Kentucky Lake or Lake Barkley, you need to make a decision. You have two options: 1) the 25-mile route to reach the Kentucky Lake-Lake Barkley Canal via the Tennessee River, with a typical three-hour delay (and it could even be longer) at Kentucky Dam; or 2) the 45-mile route that continues for 12 more miles on the Ohio River before turning off onto the Cumberland River. There is usually only a very short wait at the Lake Barkley Lock on the Cumberland River. If your boat normally cruises at seven miles per hour or faster, you could likely be in Kentucky Lake sooner via the longer Ohio-Cumberland River route. We based this estimate on the assumption that the wait before the locking will be three hours longer at the Kentucky Lock than at the Barkley Lock. If your vessel cruises at less than seven miles per hour, a potential three-hour-plus wait on the Tennessee River at Kentucky Lock might be offset by those extra 20 miles that are needed to travel on the Ohio and Cumberland rivers.

The Tennessee River first departs the Ohio River immediately east of downtown Paducah. There are two routes into the Tennessee River—one on either side of Owens Island. You could leave the Ohio at mile 934.5 and pass Owens Island on the RDB. Or you could depart the Ohio River one and a half miles farther upriver, at mile 932.8, and treat Owens Island like the LDB. The towboat traffic is lighter on the Ohio River side of Owens Island.

The Ohio River upriver from Paducah makes a gradual 90-degree curve from an east-southeast to a north-northeast heading. In this curving area, there is a concrete ramp, without a dock, at mile 928.6 on the LDB.

Ten miles past the Ohio's second confluence with the Tennessee River, the Cumberland River dumps into the Ohio. Heading up the Ohio and from a distance away, it is a bit tricky sighting the entrance to the Cumberland River. Our GPS way point, 37.07.07N/88.25.91W, might help you. There are three islands near the mouth of the Cumberland River. If you are continuing up the Ohio River to Louisville or Cincinnati, all three islands should be treated like the LDB. If you are turning into the Cumberland River, only the southernmost island, Towhead Island, should also be treated like the LDB. But the second island, Cumberland Island, should be treated like the RDB near Ohio River mile 922.8.

Towhead Island has some large mooring cells on the northwest side. Keep those large mooring cells to your southeast when entering the Cumberland River. We explored the backside, or southeast side, of Towhead Island. There are relatively high banks on both sides of the channel, and we would recommend this area as an anchorage. Entering, we remained in the center of the channel behind Towhead Island and on a heading of 55 to 60 degrees. We found no less than 12 feet of water holding almost all the way to the northeastern tip of Towhead Island. The deepest water is slightly closer to the southeastern shore and opposite the Towhead Island side. We would not recommend going around the northeast end of Towhead Island to reach the Cumberland River. We found only a few feet of water in this area. There are also treacherous rock dikes northeast of Towhead Island. If you use this anchorage, we recommend you depart it the same way you entered it—from the southwest of the island. And don't forget to turn on an anchor light at night. Nevertheless, this is perhaps the most pleasant anchorage since the Diversion Channel south of Cape Girardeau about 110 miles ago.

As you enter the Cumberland River, Cumberland Island should be treated like the RDB. Kentucky Chute is the area northeast of two-mile-long Cumberland Island. The chute reconnects to the waters of the Ohio. We explored Kentucky Chute and found the water depths fluky, and there are dikes in this area. We would not recommend the chute for navigation nor for an anchorage area.

Smithland Lock and Dam, one of the newer lock and dams on the Ohio River, was built in 1980. This lock and dam is about one mile north of Cumberland Island and can be seen from Kentucky Chute. If you wish to learn about the Ohio River north of the Smithland Lock and Dam, *Quimby's 2001 Cruising Guide* will help you.

The junction daymark at the Ohio and Cumberland rivers

CHAPTER 14

The Lower Cumberland River and Lower Lake Barkley

The narrow Cumberland River snakes its way for 31 miles before reaching the Lake Barkley Lock and Dam. Going upriver, the Cumberland generally starts heading east, then north, then east again, and then south before reaching the lock and dam at mile 30.6. The navigational aids on shore and the few floating buoys on the Cumberland River correspond remarkably well to the indicated locations on the Corps of Engineers charts. Furthermore, the Cumberland River chartbook series, produced by the Nashville District of the Corps of Engineers, is considerably better than the Ohio, and especially the Mississippi River, series. Similar to going up the Ohio River, the LDB going up the Cumberland River is on your *right*.

It is 45 miles, or 20 miles longer via the Ohio-Cumberland River route, from Paducah to the western exit of the canal to Kentucky Lake from lower Lake Barkley. Our drawing depicts the lower portions of both the Cumberland and Tennessee rivers (the Tennessee River is covered in the next chapter). Many recreational boaters opt to make the trip into Kentucky Lake via the Cumberland River instead of the shorter route on the Tennessee River. The primary reason for taking this longer route is to avoid the oftentimes long delays at Kentucky Lock and Dam on the Tennessee River. A typical waiting period for a recreational boat at Kentucky Lock might be around three hours. We have even heard of waits as long as 10 hours.

The hamlet of Smithland, Kentucky is across from Kentucky Chute on the Cumberland River. There are next to no commercial establishments in Smithland. A large new concrete boat ramp, but without a dock, can be seen at mile 2.3 on the LDB in Smithland.

During the shameful forced dislocation of many eastern Indians, which was known as the "Trail of Tears," many Cherokee Indians had to spend the brutal winter of 1838-39 in Smithland, Kentucky. Small amounts of gold had been discovered in north Georgia and eastern Tennessee in the late 1820s, and the newcomer settlers wanted it. By this time, an estimated 15,000-17,000 Cherokees lived in this area and they had adopted many of the American mores. They were farmers and ranchers, and also built schools, churches, and roads.

During the roundup and subsequent forced 1,000-mile march from as far as North Carolina, the Cherokees were routinely fleeced by the landowners of the territories through which they passed, and an estimated 3,000 to 4,000 died before reaching the arid Oklahoma Territory. The Creek, the Choctaw, the Seminoles, and the Chickasaws were included in this "Great Removal" plan to Oklahoma. Our Native Americans had a few supporters in Washington, like Daniel Webster, Henry Clay, Sam Houston, John Quincy Adams, and especially Davy Crockett. But the supporters lost. A U.S. general, General Wool, resigned his command in protest, rather than be an accessory to this

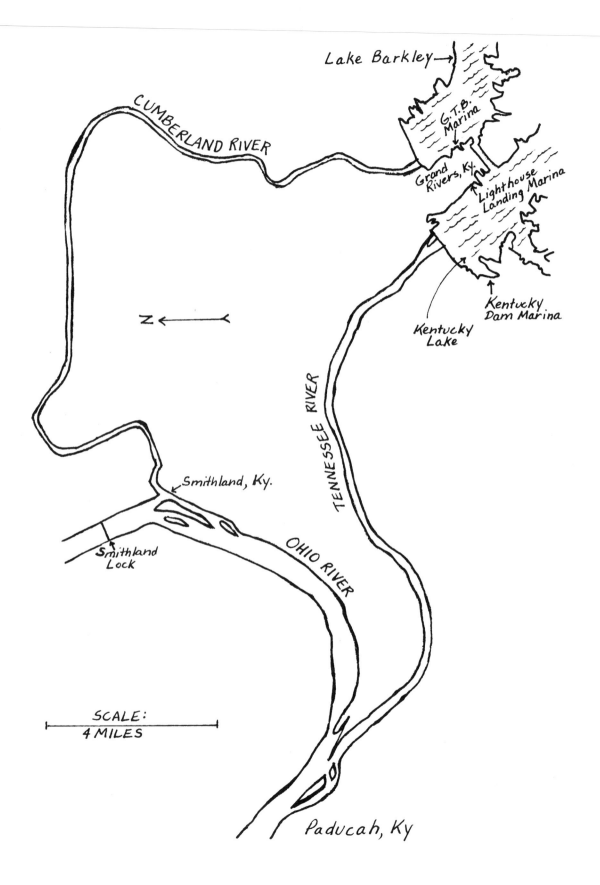

"Trail of Tears" disgrace. Tennessee Congressman Davy Crockett's political career was ruined in large part because he sided with the Cherokees. After being politically rebuked by his fellow Tennesseans, Crockett departed Tennessee for Texas. Soon afterward, Davy met his fate at the Alamo.

The U.S. Route 60 bridge crosses the Cumberland River near mile 2.8. The narrowness, steep banks, and ravinelike nature of this part of the Cumberland River are an abrupt change from the flat floodplain shores of the Ohio or Mississippi rivers. The current on the Cumberland River is about a half-knot less than on the Ohio River. There is a small barge fleeting area between river miles 5 and 6. This may be the most likely area to encounter towboat traffic.

None of the ramps on this part of the lower Cumberland River have docks. The first ramp after Smithland is at mile 10.9 on the LDB. Ramps were seen on both sides of the river at miles 15.9 and 19.7. Dycusburg, a small residential hamlet, is also at mile 19.7 on the RDB. There is another ramp at Iuka at mile 26.1 on the LDB. The Interstate 24 Bridge crosses the Cumberland at mile 27.7 and U.S. Route 62 crosses at mile 30. There is another ramp at mile 30.1 on the RDB in the pool below the massive Lake Barkley Dam. The following table lists the bridges, locks, and major river confluences covered in this chapter.

BRIDGE NAME	TYPE	VERTICAL CLEARANCE (FEET)		APPROX RIVER MILE
		normal pool	regulated high water	
Confluence with Ohio River				0.0
U.S. Route 60, Smithland	Fixed	86	43	2.8
Interstate 24	Fixed	94	40	27.7
U.S. Route 62	Fixed	90	35	30.0
Illinois Central Railroad	Fixed	95	40	30.6
Lake Barkley Lock and Dam	Lock			30.6
Route 453 over Canal to Kentucky Lake, center span	Fixed	67	51	32.8
U.S. Route 68, under the higher LDB side	Fixed	57	41	63.1

The lower Cumberland River

Perhaps, the most impressive lock and dam on this entire trip is the Lake Barkley Lock and Dam. This lock, built in 1963, has a 57-foot lift or drop and is 800 feet long. The dam is on the RDB while the lock is on the LDB, at mile 30.6. Once the pit starts adjusting, either up or down, it only takes about 12 minutes for the entire lock to fill or drain! And there is very little turbulence anywhere in this pit when either is happening. Lake Barkley Lock has an ample number of floating bollards—a total of 14. There is also much less commercial tow traffic through here than through Kentucky Lock. You can contact Lake Barkley Lock on VHF 13 or 16. Thereafter, the lock tender prefers to switch the radio traffic to

VHF channel 12. The telephone number is (270) 362-4222.

Once you are lifted out of the locking pit, and the gates open, you will be arriving upon spectacular Lake Barkley. One of the most accommodating marinas on this entire trip is Green Turtle Bay Marina. It is in the second cove on the LDB and the entrance is about one mile from the Lake Barkley Lock, at mile 31.7. Besides 450 slips and a myriad of accommodations, Green Turtle Bay has two travel lifts. A 70-ton open-ended travel lift is the larger one. Green Turtle Bay is also the only marina before the free-flowing canal that connects Lake Barkley and Kentucky Lake. It is about a mile walk from the marina to Grand Rivers, Kentucky (the marina also offers a courtesy car). This is an upscale tourist town with antique shops, a grocery store, post office, and three fine-dining restaurants.

Green Turtle Bay Marina

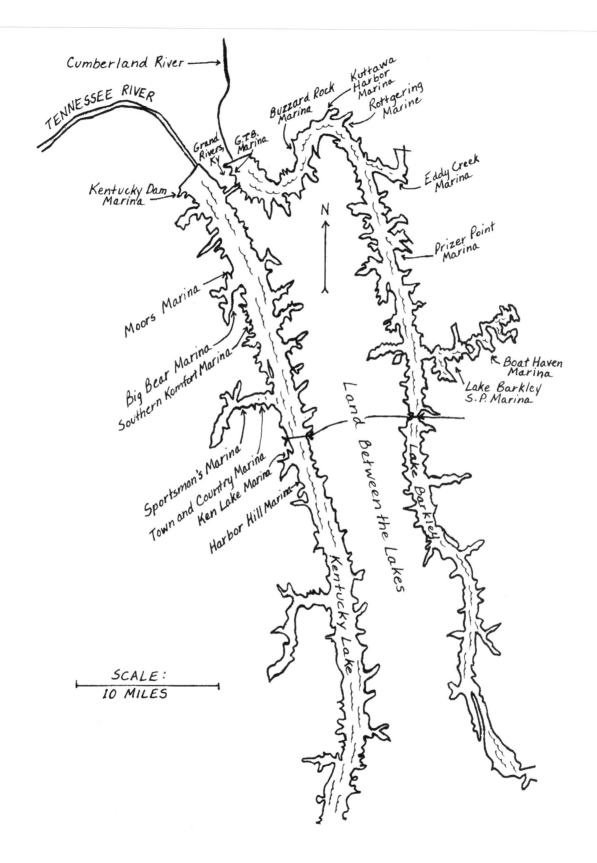

Cumberland River →

TENNESSEE RIVER

Buzzard Rock Marina

Kuttawa Harbor Marina

Rottgering Marine

Grand Rivers, Ky.

G.T.B. Marina

Kentucky Dam Marina

Eddy Creek Marina

N

Prizer Point Marina

Moors Marina

Big Bear Marina

Southern Komfort Marina

Boat Haven Marina

Lake Barkley S.P. Marina

Land Between the Lakes

Sportsman's Marina

Town and Country Marina

Ken Lake Marina

Harbor Hill Marina

Lake Barkley

Kentucky Lake

SCALE:
10 MILES

Patti's 1880's Settlement is perhaps the most renowned restaurant in town. Our next drawing depicts much of Lake Barkley and a portion of Kentucky Lake (covered in chapter 15).

Green Turtle Bay Marina (270) 362-8364, VHF 10
http://www.greenturtlebay.com

Approach depth—10 feet
Dockside depth—10 feet
Accepts transients—yes
Floating concrete docks—yes
Dockside power connections—30 and twin
   50 amp
Dockside water connections—yes
Waste pump-out—yes
Showers—yes
Laundromat—yes
Gasoline—yes
Diesel fuel—yes
Mechanical repairs—yes
Below-waterline repairs—yes
Ship's and convenience store—yes
Restaurant—on site at yacht club and several
   nearby

If you are in Lake Barkley and wish to continue on the Great Circle, you must connect to Kentucky Lake via the one-and-a-half-mile-long canal at mile 32.7 on the LDB. The highway bridge over the canal has a vertical clearance of about 67 feet at pool stage and about 51 feet at the regulated high water stage. There are at least another half-dozen marinas farther upstream on Lake Barkley. Beyond this canal, the LDB of Lake Barkley is the "Land Between the Lakes," or LBL. It was created in 1963 with the construction of the Lake Barley Dam. The 170,000-acre narrow peninsula has more than 300 miles of shoreline. The area is rich in natural beauty and wildlife, with a 750-acre elk and buffalo prairie and 200 miles of hiking trails. After the free-flowing canal section, the Land Between the Lakes is approximately eight miles wide by 40 miles long.

After nearly 40 miles of lakelike proportions, Lake Barkley chokes down to the Cumberland River again. The river bends its way east and then even slightly north. Nashville is the biggest city on the Cumberland River, and it is about 160 miles from the Barkley Lock and Dam. Celina, Tennessee, the head of navigation on the Cumberland River, is 350 miles upriver from the Barkley Lock.

We visited a few marinas on the lower, or northern, portion of Lake Barkley. Buzzard Rock, Eddy Creek, Kuttawa Harbor, and Prizer Point marinas are the largest in this area, and each has at least 150 slips. Lake Barkley State Park and Boat Haven marinas have between 90 and 120 slips. Rottgering is a haul-out facility and working yard with a 50-ton open-ended travel lift. The marinas all have boat ramps and there are dozens of other boat ramps in this part of Lake Barkley.

In Poplar Creek, mile 39.4, RDB:

Buzzard Rock Marina and Resort (270) 388-
   7925

Approach depth—10+ feet
Accepts transients—yes
Floating steel docks—yes
Dockside power connections—30 and 50 amp
Dockside water connections—yes
Waste pump-out—yes
Showers—yes
Laundromat—yes
Gasoline—yes

Mechanical repairs—yes
Below-waterline repairs—yes
Ship's store—yes
Café—yes

In Hammond Creek, mile 42.0, RDB:

Kuttawa Harbor Marina
   (270) 388-9563

Approach depth—9 feet
Accepts transients—limited
Floating concrete docks—yes
Dockside power connections—15 and
   30 amp
Dockside water connections—yes
Waste pump-out—yes
Gasoline—yes
Diesel fuel—yes
Variety store—yes
Restaurant—on site

In Lick Creek, mile 43.0, RDB:

Rottgering Marine (270) 388-0360

Approach depth—12 feet
Mechanical repairs—yes
Below-waterline repairs—yes

In Eddy Creek, mile 46.5, RDB:

Eddy Creek Marina Resort
   (270) 388-2271
http://www.eddycreek.com/

Approach depth—12 feet
Accepts transients—yes
Floating concrete docks—yes
Dockside power connections—30 and
   50 amp
Dockside water connections—yes
Waste pump-out—yes
Showers—yes
Laundromat—yes
Gasoline—yes
Diesel fuel—yes

Mechanical repairs—yes
Ship's store—yes
Restaurant—on site

In Hurricane Creek, mile 54.7, RDB:

Prizer Point Marina and Resort
   (270) 522-3762
http://www.prizerpoint.com

Approach depth—20 feet
Dockside depth—12 feet
Accepts transients—yes
Floating concrete docks—yes
Dockside power connections—30 and
   50 amp
Dockside water connections—yes
Waste pump-out—yes
Showers—yes
Laundromat—yes
Gasoline—yes
Diesel fuel—yes
Mechanical repairs—yes
Below-waterline repairs—yes
Ship's and variety store—yes
Restaurant—on site

In Little River, mile 59.0, RDB:

Lake Barkley State Park Marina
   (270) 924-9954

Approach depth—18 feet
Dockside depth—5 feet
Accepts transients—yes
Floating wooden piers—yes
Dockside power connections—30 and
   50 amp
Dockside water connections—yes
Waste pump-out—yes
Showers—yes
Laundromat—yes
Gasoline—yes
Diesel fuel—yes
Ship's store—yes
Restaurant—on site

Boat Haven Resort and Marina
   (270) 522-7638

Approach depth—10 feet
Accepts transients—limited
Floating concrete docks—yes
Dockside water connections—yes
Showers—yes
Gasoline—yes
Ship's store—yes (limited)
Restaurant—on site

If you wish to learn about Cumberland River marinas farther upriver, Fred Myers' *Cumberland River Cruise Guide* or *Quimby's 2001 Cruising Guide* should help you.

A fleet of tied towboats on the Tennessee River

CHAPTER 15

The Lower Tennessee River and Lower Kentucky Lake

The Tennessee River dumps into the Ohio River near downtown Paducah, Kentucky and at Tennessee River mile 0. Review the first drawing in chapter 14. There are two navigable routes in or out of the Tennessee River—one on either side of Owens Island. Our GPS way point, 37.04.70N/88.34.20W, is at the eastern end of Owens Island, and more upriver on the Ohio River. This way point is near Tennessee River mile 2.3. Using this more eastern approach route into the main Tennessee River, you should find less towboat traffic on the Ohio River side of Owens Island. But beware of some large sand bars that are east of Owens Island. On the south side of Owens Island and east of Paducah, there are several busy towboat docks near the channel. With either route into the Tennessee River, you should treat the Cuba Towhead Island like the LDB.

Like on the neighboring Cumberland River, the shoreside navigational aids and buoys on the Tennessee River correspond very well to their locations on the Nashville District Corps of Engineers charts. The Tennessee River is much wider than the Cumberland. It has a bit more industry and barge traffic too, especially in the lowest portions. We encountered about a knot of current on the lower part of the Tennessee River.

It is 25 miles from Paducah to the western exit of the free-flowing canal between Lake Barkley and Kentucky Lake via the Tennessee River (and lower Kentucky Lake). Soon after you enter the Tennessee, you will see floating dry docks, used for barge repair, on the LDB before the U.S. Route 60 Bridge. This highway bridge crosses the Tennessee at mile 5.3. The heaviest concentration of barge staging is south of this bridge. The barge traffic lightens upriver from the bridge.

There are two concrete boat ramps on both sides of the river near mile 16.4, and neither ramp has a dock. This was likely an old ferryboat crossing. There is a power-plant substation and an industrial complex near Calvert City between river miles 16.8 and 18.3 on the LDB. Despite the industrial flavor, we saw hundreds of turtles basking on the banks and on the woody debris near the shore of the Tennessee River. The Interstate 24 Bridge crosses the Tennessee River at mile 21.1. The following table lists the bridges, locks, and major river confluences covered in this chapter.

BRIDGE NAME	TYPE	VERTICAL CLEARANCE (FEET)		APPROX RIVER MILE
		normal pool	regulated high water	
Confluence with Ohio River, Paducah				0.0
U.S. Route 60, Paducah	Fixed	84	47	5.3
Interstate 24 & Illinois Central Railroad	Fixed	87	45	21.1
U.S. Route 62	Fixed	85	48	22.4
Kentucky Lock and Dam	Lock			22.4
Route 453 over Canal to Lake Barkley, center span	Fixed	67	51	32.8
U.S. Route 68	Fixed	57	41	41.7

Kentucky Lock and Dam is 22 miles from Paducah. It is considerably older than the Lake Barkley Lock and Dam, and it is inherently less efficient. This lock and dam, like many of the Tennessee Valley Authority, was built during Franklin Roosevelt's New Deal era.

Furthermore, Kentucky Lock must handle much more commercial tow traffic than the Lake Barkley Lock. We have heard that a typical wait for recreational vessels is three hours. We have heard of layovers as long as seven hours and even longer. We went through this lock twice, and both times the commercial traffic was light, but we still had a wait outside of the pit for between three and four hours. If your vessel is not slower than seven mph, the Ohio-Cumberland River route to Kentucky Lake, albeit 20 miles longer, will probably be the faster route.

Like the Lake Barkley Lock, the lift or drop here is 57 feet. The dam is on the LDB while the lock is on the RDB. There is also an interesting TVA lock visitor center on the RDB, which is next to the lock and accessed by land from the downriver side. Kentucky Lock tenders monitor VHF 13 and 16 and prefer to shift radio traffic to channel 14. The phone number is (270) 362-4226. There are floating bollards in the Kentucky Lock but fewer functioning bollards than in the Lake Barkley Lock. There is more turbulence in the Kentucky Lock as well. The turbulence is negligible when locking down; but when locking up, you may find less turbulence at the forward end of the lock. Whether locking up or down, the lock master will usually indicate over the VHF radio where you should tie up.

Once you are out of the locking pit and on beautiful Kentucky Lake, options are plentiful. Two marinas are close to the lock. Kentucky Dam Marina, with about 350 slips and a lodge on the premises, is on the LDB at mile 22.9. There is a well-marked channel leading to the opening in the offset breakwater wall, which houses Kentucky Dam Marina in Taylor Creek. Lighthouse Landing Marina, a sailboat marina with about 200 slips, is on the RDB at mile 24.1. Lighthouse Landing Marina and Green

Kentucky Lock opening after a three-hour wait to lock up

Kentucky Lock opening after locking down

Turtle Bay Marina (on the nearby Lake Barkley) are popular places to have sailboat masts stepped or unstepped. By land, Lighthouse Landing Marina is only about a third of a mile from all of the fancy shops and restaurants in Grand Rivers, Kentucky. Both Lighthouse Landing and Kentucky Dam marinas are located prior to the canal that connects Kentucky Lake to Lake Barkley at mile 25.3.

After the free-flowing canal, there are more than a dozen marinas on Kentucky Lake, all of them on the LDB. After the Lake Barkley Canal, the RDB of Kentucky Lake is the "Land Between the Lakes." The Land Between the Lakes, a brainchild of the Kennedy administration, was to be a unique model portraying how an area with limited industrial, agricultural, and forestry resources could still have a stimulating economy—and an economy based on outdoor recreation. The idea sure seems to have worked. Please review the second chapter 14 drawing for Kentucky Lake and the area around the Land Between the Lakes.

Kentucky Dam Marina (270) 362-8386
http://www.kentuckylake.com/kdm

Approach depth—15 feet
Dockside depth—10 feet
Accepts transients—yes
Floating concrete and wooden docks—yes
Dockside power connections—15, 30, and 50 amp
Dockside water connections—yes
Waste pump-out—yes
Showers—accessible with courtesy car
Laundromat—accessible with courtesy car
Gasoline—yes
Diesel fuel—yes
Mechanical repairs—yes
Ship's store—yes (limited)
Restaurant—accessible with courtesy car

Lighthouse Landing Marina (270) 362-8201
http://www.lighthouselanding.com

Approach depth—9 feet
Accepts transients—yes, prefers sailboats
Floating steel and wooden docks—yes
Dockside power connections—20 and 30 amp
Dockside water connections—yes
Waste pump-out—yes
Showers—yes
Laundromat—yes
Mechanical repairs—limited, no engine repairs
Below-waterline repairs—yes
Ship's store—yes
Restaurant—several nearby

A well-marked secondary channel hangs close to the LDB of Kentucky Lake. It starts at Kentucky Dam Marina in Taylor Creek and terminates 43 miles away at Paris Landing State Park in Tennessee. This channel is marked by smaller-than-usual nun and can buoys with white-painted tops.

Instead of following the main channel, we traveled this more picturesque secondary channel for 28 miles and had no problems. There are more than a dozen connecting channels between this and the main channel. Although more attention is needed to navigate this secondary channel than the main channel, the secondary channel has quicker and easier access to the many creeks and marinas on the LDB of Kentucky Lake. We usually found no less than seven feet of water in this secondary channel.

Following are some of the larger marinas that we visited on the lowest portion—the northern 20 miles—of Kentucky Lake. In many of the smaller tributaries on Kentucky Lake, and even in the area where we researched, there are several more, but smaller marinas. There are also no less than a score of boat ramps in this northern section of Kentucky Lake.

In Bear Creek, mile 31.4, or mile 7.3 on secondary, LDB:

Moors Resort and Marina (270) 362-8361
http://www.moorsresort.com/

Approach depth—9 feet
Accepts transients—yes
Floating concrete and wooden docks—yes
Dockside power connections—30 amp
Dockside water connections—yes
Waste pump-out—yes
Showers—yes
Laundromat—yes
Gasoline—yes
Ship's store—yes
Restaurant—on site

Big Bear Resort and Marina (270) 354-6414
http://www.bigbearkentuckylake.com/

Approach depth—6 feet
Accepts transients—yes
Floating wooden piers—yes (covered)
Dockside power connections—30 amp
Dockside water connections—yes
Waste pump-out—yes
Showers—yes
Laundromat—yes
Gasoline—yes
Ship's store—yes

In mouth of creek at mile 33.1, or mile 9.9 on secondary, LDB:

Southern Komfort Marina and Resort (270) 354-6422

Approach depth—12 feet
Accepts transients—yes
Floating steel and wooden docks—yes
Dockside power connections—20 and 30 amp
Dockside water connections—yes

Waste pump-out—yes
Showers—yes
Laundromat—yes
Gasoline—yes

In Jonathan Creek, mile 36.7, or mile 15.1 on secondary, LDB:

Town and Country Marina (270) 354-8828

Approach depth—4 feet
Accepts transients—yes
Floating wooden piers—yes
Dockside power connections—30 and 50 amp
Dockside water connections—yes
Showers—yes
Laundromat—yes
Gasoline—yes
Mechanical repairs—yes (independent
    contractor)
Ship's store—yes
Restaurant—on site

Sportsman's Anchor Marina (270) 354-6568
http://www.kentuckylake.com/anchor

Approach depth—6-8 feet
Accepts transients—yes
Floating wooden piers—yes (covered)
Dockside power connections—limited
Laundromat—yes
Gasoline—yes
Mechanical repairs—yes
Ship's store—yes
Restaurant—nearby

In Ledbetter Creek, mile 42.1, or mile 19.4 on secondary, LDB:

KenLake Marina (270) 474-2245

Approach depth—11 feet
Dockside depth—11 feet
Accepts transients—yes
Floating concrete docks—yes
Dockside power connections—30 and 50 amp
Dockside water connections—yes

Waste pump-out—yes
Gasoline—yes
Diesel fuel—yes
Mechanical repairs—yes (independent
contractor)
Ship's store—yes
Restaurant—on site

In creek at mile 44.1, or mile 22.7 on secondary, LDB:

Harbor Hill Marina (270) 474-2228

Approach depth—20 feet
Dockside depth—4 feet
Accepts transients—yes
Floating wooden piers—yes
Dockside power connections—30 and 50 amp
Mechanical repairs—yes
Below-waterline repairs—yes

Moors Marina had a horrible fire on October 18, 2000, a few days before we visited, in which about 35 boats and one entire pier were lost. We wish them our best as they rebuild. Moors, Southern Komfort, and KenLake marinas have reasonably quick access to the main body of the Kentucky Lake. Each has over 100 slips and can accommodate fairly large boats (at least 45 to 60 footers). Sportsman's Anchor Marina, with about 170 slips, is about three miles from the main body of the lake. Big Bear Marina, with about 110 slips, and Town and Country Marina, with about 200 slips, are both about two miles from the main body of Kentucky Lake. Harbor Hill Marina has only about 20 slips, and it is more a working yard, with a 20-ton

lift, than a full-service marina. Nevertheless, Bill, the owner, plans to build a new and larger marina facility in the creek to the north, in an area near Pacer Point.

Kentucky Lake is huge and maintains its wide proportions for 77 miles. It narrows somewhat after mile marker 100 and perhaps looks more like the "predammed" Tennessee River. Near Tennessee River mile 206, you'd lock into Pickwick Landing Lake. In that lake, at mile 215, Yellow Creek branches off the LDB. Yellow Creek is the start of the Tennessee-Tombigbee Waterway. This is also near the point where the states of Tennessee, Mississippi, and Alabama come together.

On the way to Mobile, Alabama, the 1985 Tenn-Tom Waterway passes some enchanting areas. Mobile is 450 miles from Pickwick Landing Lake and 642 miles from the Kentucky Lock on the Tennessee River. Review the second diagram in chapter 3 for the locks between Kentucky Lake and the Gulf of Mexico. If you decided to remain on the Tennessee River after Pickwick Landing Lake, the city of Chattanooga is another 250 miles upriver. Knoxville, near the head of Tennessee River navigation, is about 440 miles up the river from the lake.

You can learn more about the Tennessee River or the Tenn-Tom Waterway marinas and services by reading Fred Myers' *Tennessee River Cruise Guide*, Fred Myers' *Tenn-Tom Nitty-Gritty Cruise Guide*, or *Quimby's 2001 Cruising Guide*.

Acknowledgments and Dedication

After Ecuador, the malaria, and my shoulder operation, and then after my van was totaled by a red-light-running postal vehicle, this sore ex-Peace Corps volunteer's options for sleeping quarters were rather limited. I thank Jim Fitzsimmons, Carlton Shufflebarger, Stitch Wilson, the Durham family, and a few others for opening up their homes to me. I also thank Claiborne Young for the enlightenment and the magnanimous support throughout the research and writing of this guide.

Like any researcher and guide writer, I'm indebted to many others. I thank the folks who dropped their planned schedules to help me trailer the Nimble Nomad around. Nimble dealer Cliff Stoneburner helped me get started by trailering my Nomad from Annapolis to Chicago. In Columbus, Georgia, where this trip eventually terminated, Wes, Bubba, and the other folks at Action Marine were of great help trailering the Nomad back to Maryland. I'd like to thank the professional Cape Girardeau, Missouri towboat *Volunteer,* who quickly came to our aid and towed us out of harm's way when our engine failed one foggy morning on the Mississippi River.

In the late innings, a few people reviewed and improved this guide. Ray Beth Durham, Fred Lierley, Ralph and Janis Fischer, Townsend Goddard, and especially my father added some new ideas and contributed some polish. Pat Champagne deserves special recognition. On short notice, she was able to artistically draw 21 area charts from raw data and very sketchy inputs. Thanks a million, Pat. Bill Lipovsky helped me cull many of the photographs. In the early innings, I also especially thank Fred Lierley. As we were researching on the rivers, Fred, with his genuine folksy manner, was a pleasant and disarming contrast to my business-first approach. He was always the optimist. When something not so good occurred on these rivers, and it occasionally did, I'd tighten up. After the crisis, and with Fred's critical help "putting out the fire," he had a great way of saying, "Well, that wasn't so bad." And you know . . . Fred was right.

Fellow cruisers edified us: Sam and Dawn Vaura aboard *Red Knight,* delivery captains Jim and Patty aboard *RiverSong,* and especially Joe and Betsey Butera aboard *Stina.* I'd also like to thank the real river people like Charlie and Fern Hopkins at Hoppie's Marina. To all the friendly folks at the 59th Street Harbor Marina, Crowley's Yacht Yard in Chicago, the Lake Calumet Boat and Gun Club, the South Shore Boat Club in Peru, Illinois, East Peoria Boat Club, Palisades Marina in Portage des Sioux, Green Turtle Bay in Kentucky, and all the others out there with whom we were not able to spend as much time as we had wished—thank you.

Some of us are fortunate enough to be have an opportunity to travel and sail along these great rivers. But we could not do it, at least not very well, if others didn't accommodate us with various services along the way. And there are others who maintain these rivers for us. So this guide is dedicated to them—those "River Workers."

List of U.S. Government Chart Books and Charts

NOAA Recreation Chart Book 14926: "Chicago and South Shore of Lake Michigan"—with 14 applicable pages out of a book of 30 charts

OR

Individual NOAA Charts: 14927: "Chicago Lake Front"   Scale: 1:60,000
14928: "Chicago Harbor"   Scale: 1:15,000
14929: "Calumet and Indiana Harbors"   Scale: 1:15,000

U.S. Army Corps of Engineers: "Illinois Waterway Navigation Charts," Rock Island District—with all 142 applicable pages of charts

"Upper Mississippi River Navigation Charts," Rock Island District—with 30 applicable pages out of a book of 130 charts

OR

"Mississippi River, Flood Control and Navigation Maps—below Hannibal, Missouri to the Gulf of Mexico," Mississippi Valley Division—with 21 applicable pages out of a book of 153 charts*

"Ohio River Navigation Charts," Louisville District—with 15 applicable pages out of a book of 122 charts

"Cumberland River Navigation Charts," Nashville District—with about 12 applicable pages out of a book of 62 charts

"Tennessee River Navigation Charts," Nashville District—with about 11 applicable pages out of a book of 118 charts

*This chartbook series was unavailable at the time of our research.

River Mile Location Indices

FEATURE	LOCATION	
	Mile	Bank

Mileage Markers for Marinas and Locks on the Calumet River (Chapter 6)

FEATURE	Mile	Bank
Calumet Harbor, Lake Michigan	333.5	
Confluence with the Lake Calumet Feeder Channel	327.2	RDB
Thomas O'Brien Lock	326.4	RDB
Riverside Marina	326.1	LDB
Sunset Harbor Marina	326.0	LDB
Windjammer Marina	325.8	LDB
Croissant Marina	325.6	LDB
Riley's Marina	325.4	LDB
Marine Services Corporation	324.3	LDB
Pier 11 Marina	323.3	LDB
Lake Calumet Boat and Gun Club	323.2	LDB
Skipper's Marina	322.7	RDB
Rentner's Marina	322.5	LDB
Triplex Marina	319.9	LDB
Confluence with the Chicago Sanitary & Ship Canal	303.5	RDB

Mileage Markers for Marinas and Locks on the Chicago River and Chicago Sanitary and Ship Canal (Chapter 7)

FEATURE	Mile	Bank
Chicago River Lock	327.2	
Skipper Bud's Marina City Marina	326.1	RDB
Confluence with the North Branch of the Chicago River	325.5	RDB
River City Marina	324.6	LDB
Skokie Marine Service	323.4	RDB
South Branch Marina	322.9	RDB
Crowley's Yacht Yard	322.6	LDB
Chicago Yacht Yard	321.6	RDB
Confluence with the Calumet (or Cal-Sag Channel)	303.5	LDB
Lockport Lock	291.1	LDB

Mileage Markers for Marinas, Locks, and Towns on the Des Plaines River
(Chapter 8)

Joliet, Illinois	289-87	L&RDB
Brandon Road Lock	286.0	RDB
Big Basin Marina	277.8	RDB
Three Rivers Marina	274.9	LDB
Harborside Marina	273.7	LDB
Bay Hill Marina	273.6	LDB
Confluence with the Kankakee River	272.8	LDB

Mileage Markers for Marinas, Locks, and Towns on the Upper Illinois River
(Chapter 8)

Dresden Island Lock	271.5	LDB
Morris, Illinois	263.5	RDB
Custom Marine, east basins	253.2	LDB
Blacks Marine/Boondocks Restaurant	252.8	LDB
Custom Marine, yard and store	252.7	LDB
Seneca Boat Club	252.7	RDB
Seneca, Illinois	252.7	RDB
Hidden Cove Marina	252.4	LDB
Mariner's Village and Marina	252.2	RDB
Spring Brook Marina	251.8	LDB

Mileage Markers for Marinas, Locks, and Towns on the Upper Illinois River
(Chapter 9)

Snug Harbor Marina	247.4	RDB
Marseilles, Illinois	247.3	RDB
Marseilles Lock	244.6	LDB
Four Star Marina	242.3	RDB
Ottawa, Illinois	239.7	RDB
South Ottawa, Illinois	239.7	LDB
Starved Rock Yacht Club	233.9	RDB
Starved Rock Marina	233.4	RDB
Starved Rock Lock	231.0	RDB
La Salle, Illinois	223.1	RDB
Peru, Illinois	222.1	RDB

South Shore Boat Club	222.0	RDB
Spring Valley Boat Club	218.5	LDB
Spring Valley, Illinois	218.4	RDB
Hennepin, Illinois	207.5	LDB
Henry Marina	196.1	RDB
Henry, Illinois	196.0	RDB
Morgan's Landing Marina	189.1	LDB
Lacon, Illinois	189.1	LDB
Chillicothe, Illinois	180.5	RDB
Chillicothe Condominium Marina	179.9	RDB

Mileage Markers for Marinas and Locks on Upper Peoria and Peoria Lakes
(Chapter 10)

Hamm's Holiday Harbor Marina	178.6	RDB
National Marine North Marina	169.4	RDB
Whitecap Drifters Boat Club	169.2	RDB
National Marine South Marina	168.3	RDB
Illinois Valley Yacht Club, north entry	167.8	RDB
Rainbow Cove Marina	167.7	LDB (distant)
Sodowski's Boat Club	167.6	RDB
East Peoria Boat Club	167.5	LDB (distant)
Rainbow Cove Marina	167.7	LDB (distant)
Wharf Harbor Marina	165.2	RDB (distant)
Spindler's Marina	165.2	LDB (distant)
Eastport Marina	164.0	LDB (distant)
Detweiller's Municipal Marina	163.7	RDB
Peoria Boat Club	163.7	RDB
Downtown Peoria, Illinois	162.6	RDB
Peoria Lock	157.7	LDB

Mileage Markers for Marinas, Locks, and Towns on the Lower Illinois River
(Chapter 11)

Pekin Boat Club and Trailer Park	153.1	LDB
Pekin, Illinois	152.8	LDB
Liverpool, Illinois	128.1	RDB
Havana, Illinois	120.2	LDB
River's Edge Boat Club	97.4	RDB
Beardstown, Illinois	88.6	LDB

La Grange Lock	80.2	RDB
Meredosia, Illinois (Naples Boat Club)	71.2	LDB
Kampsville, Illinois (ferry crossing)	32.1	RDB
Hardin, Illinois and Illinois Riverdock Restaurant	20.9	RDB
Pere Marquette State Park and Boat Facility	7.3	LDB
Grafton, Illinois	0.4	LDB
Confluence with the Mississippi River	0.0	RDB

Mileage Markers for Marinas, Locks, and Towns on the Mississippi River
(Chapter 12)

Confluence with the Illinois River	218.0	LDB
The four Portage des Sioux marinas	212.4	RDB
Portage des Sioux, Missouri	212.4	RDB
Small boat harbors south of Portage des Sioux	211.4	RDB
Piasa Harbor Marina (safest approach from channel)	207.2	LDB
Harbour Point Yacht Club	204.5	RDB
Alton, Illinois	203.1	LDB
Alton Marina	202.5	LDB
Melvin Price Lock or Lock Number 26	200.8	LDB
Confluence with the Missouri River	195.0	RDB
Chain of Rocks Canal, upriver entry	194.3	LDB
Chain of Rocks Lock or Lock Number 27	185.5	LDB
Chain of Rocks Canal, downriver entry	184.0	LDB
Downtown St. Louis, Missouri	179.4	RDB
Hoppie's Marina and Kimmswick, Missouri	158.5	RDB
Marina de Gabouri and Ste. Genevieve, Missouri	122.4	RDB
Confluence with the Kaskaskia River	117.5	LDB
Chester, Illinois	110.0	LDB
Anchorage northwest of Rockwood Island	102.4	LDB
Cape Girardeau, Missouri (Kidd's Fuel Dock)	51.9	RDB
Anchorage, Little River Diversion Channel	48.8	RDB
Anchorage southeast of Boston Bar	7.6	LDB
Anchorage east of Angelo Towhead	1.5	LDB
Confluence with the Ohio River	0.0	LDB

Mileage Markers for Marinas, Locks, and Towns on the Ohio River
(Chapter 13)

| Confluence with the Mississippi River | 981.5 | RDB |

Cairo, Illinois	979.2	RDB
Future City, Illinois	977.0	RDB
Mound City, Illinois	973.0	RDB
Olmsted Lock (under construction)	964.6	RDB
Lock 53	962.6	RDB
Joppa, Illinois	951.4	RDB
Metropolis, Illinois	942.2	RDB
Lock 52	939.0	RDB
Big E Marina	935.1	LDB
Downtown Paducah, Kentucky	934.5	LDB
Confluence with the Tennessee River:		
Northwest of Owens Island	934.5	LDB
East of Owens Island	932.8	LDB
Anchorage southeast of Towhead Island	923.5	LDB
Confluence with the Cumberland River	923.0	LDB
Smithland Lock	918.7	RDB

Mileage Markers for Marinas, Locks, and Towns on the Lower Cumberland River
(Chapter 14)

Confluence with the Ohio River	0.0	RDB
Kentucky Chute	2.2	RDB
Smithland, Kentucky	2.3	LDB
Barkley Lock	30.4	LDB
Green Turtle Bay Marina and Grand Rivers, Kentucky	31.7	LDB
Confluence with the Kentucky Lake Canal	32.7	LDB
Buzzard Rock Marina and Resort	39.4	RDB
Kuttawa Harbor Marina	42.0	RDB
Rottgering Marine	43.0	RDB
Eddy Creek Marina and Resort	46.5	RDB
Prizer Point Marina and Resort	54.7	RDB
Lake Barkley State Park Marina	59.0	RDB
Boat Haven Resort and Marina	59.0	RDB (distant)

Mileage Markers for Marinas, Locks, and Towns on the Lower Tennessee River
(Chapter 15)

Paducah, Kentucky	0.0	LDB

Confluence with the Ohio River:

Northwest of Owens Island	0.0	RDB
East of Owens Island	2.2	RDB
Kentucky Lock	22.4	RDB
Kentucky Dam Marina	22.9	LDB
Lighthouse Landing Marina and Grand Rivers, Kentucky	24.1	RDB
Confluence with the Lake Barkley Canal	25.3	RDB
Moors Resort and Marina	31.4	LDB
Big Bear Resort and Marina	31.4	LDB (distant)
Southern Komfort Marina and Resort	33.1	LDB
Town and Country Marina	36.7	LDB
Sportsman Anchor Marina	36.7	LDB (distant)
KenLake Marina	42.1	LDB
Harbor Hill Marine	44.1	LDB
Pickwick Landing Lock, and beginning of the lake	206.7	LDB
Confluence with Yellow Creek, and the beginning of the Tenn-Tom Waterway	215.1	LDB

GPS Location Indices

FEATURE	GPS WAY POINT
Way Points for Lake Michigan (Chapter 5)	
Outside Montrose Harbor Marina	41.57.50N/87.37.80W
Outside Belmont Harbor Marina	41.56.40N/87.37.80W
Outside Diversey Harbor Marina	41.55.95N/87.37.75W
Outside the pass in breakwater wall near Chicago River	41.53.29N/87.35.36W
Outside Monroe Harbor Marina (and Du Sable Harbor)	41.52.41N/87.36.48W
Outside Burnham Park Harbor Marina	41.50.89N/87.36.34W
Outside 59th Street Harbor Marina	41.47.31N/87.34.30W
Outside Jackson Park Outer Harbor Marinas	41.46.86N/87.33.92W
Outside the pass in breakwater wall of Calumet Harbor	41.44.24N/87.30.18W
Outside Hammond Marina	41.41.70N/87.30.10W
Way Points for Upper Peoria Lake (Chapter 10)	
On the RDB and just outside of the main channel:	
For National Marine North Marina	40.46.22N/89.33.69W
For Whitecap Drifters Boat Club	40.46.15N/89.33.62W
For National Marine South Marina	40.45.21N/89.33.38W
For Illinois Valley Yacht Club, north entry	40.44.90N/89.33.17W
For Sodowski's Boat Club	40.44.80N/89.33.22W
On the LDB and well outside of the main channel:	
For Rainbow Cove Marina	40.44.91N/89.32.26W
For East Peoria Boat Club	40.44.78N/89.32.38W
Way Points Outside the Main Channel for Peoria Lake (Chapter 10)	
For Wharf Harbor Marina (on the RDB)	40.42.67N/89.33.08W
For Spindler's Marina (on the LDB)	40.42.65N/89.32.67W
For Detweiller's Municipal Marina (on the RDB)	40.41.91N/89.34.06W
For Eastport Marina (on the LDB)	40.41.84N/89.33.30W

Some Way Points on the Mississippi River (Chapter 12)

Outside the channel (on the RDB) to the four Portage des Sioux marinas	38.56.02N/90.20.16W
Outside the channel (on the LDB) to Piasa Harbor north entry for shallow-draft vessels only	38.55.57N/90.19.37W
Outside the channel (on the LDB) to Piasa Harbor south entry for most vessels	38.55.36N/90.14.77W
Outside the channel (on the RDB) for Harbour Point Yacht Club	38.53.81N/90.12.41W
Chain of Rocks Canal (on the LDB) north entry	38.47.80N/90.07.20W
Chain of Rocks Canal (on the LDB) south entry	38.40.68N/90.11.21W

Some Other Notable Way Points

At the junction of the Calumet and Chicago canals	41.41.81N/87.56.95W
At the junction of the Des Plaines and Kankakee rivers (i.e., the head of the Illinois River)	41.23.63N/88.15.42W
At the junction of the Illinois and Mississippi rivers	38.57.80N/90.25.60W
At the junction of the Ohio and Mississippi rivers	36.59.13N/89.07.80W
At the junction of the Tennessee and Ohio rivers	37.04.70N/88.34.20W
At the junction of the Cumberland and Ohio rivers	37.07.07N/88.25.91W

Bibliography

Derleth, August. *Vincennes: Portal to the West.* Englewood Cliffs, N.J.: Prentice-Hall, 1968.

Gray, James. *The Illinois.* New York: J. J. Little and Ives Company, 1940.

Jahoda, Gloria. *The Trail of Tears.* New York: Random House, 1995.

Lloyd, Alan. *Great Circle Navigation Notes.* Milford, Ohio, 2000.

McDermott, John Francis. *The French in the Mississippi Valley.* Urbana, Ill.: University of Illinois Press, 1965.

Myers, Fred. *Tennessee River Cruise Guide.* Jacksonville, Fla.: Hartley Press, 1998.

Myers, Fred. *Tenn-Tom Nitty-Gritty Cruise Guide.* Jacksonville, Fla.: Hartley Press, 2001.

O'Meara, Walter B. *Lakeland Boating Lake Michigan Port O'Call.* Evanston, Ill.: O'Meara-Brown Publications, 1998.

Spencer, H. Nelson. *Quimby's 2001 Cruising Guide.* St. Louis, Mo.: Waterway Journal, 2001.

U.S. Coast Pilot, vol. 6, *Great Lakes.* Annapolis, Md.: Prostar Publications, 2001.

Wattenberg, Ben. *Busy Waterways.* New York: John Day, 1964.

Index

For More Cruising Guides

Other Cruising Guides from Pelican Publishing Company

Power Cruising, by Claiborne S. Young
Cruising Guide to Eastern Florida, by Claiborne S. Young
Cruising Guide to Western Florida, by Claiborne S. Young
Cruising Guide to the Northern Gulf Coast, by Claiborne S. Young
Cruising Guide to New York Waterways and Lake Champlain, by Chris W. Brown III

Other Cruising Guides by Capt. Rick Rhodes

Discovering the Tidal Potomac. Heron Island Media, 1998.
Honduras and Its Bay Islands. Heron Island Media, 1998.